A MIDLIFE WOMAN

A WOMAN LOST

BOOK ELEVEN

T.B. MARKINSON

LET'S KEEP IN TOUCH

One of the best parts of publishing is getting to know *you*, the reader.

My favorite method of keeping in touch is via my newsletter, where I share about my writing life, my cat (whom I lovingly call the Demon Cat since she hissed at me for the first forty-eight hours after I adopted her), upcoming new releases, promotions, and giveaways.

And, I give away two e-books to two newsletter subscribers every month. The winners will be able to choose from my backlist or an upcoming release.

I love giving back to you, which is why if you join my newsletter, I'll send you a free e-copy of *A Woman Lost*, book 1 of the A Woman Lost series, and bonus chapters you can't get anywhere else.

Also, you'll receive a free e-copy of *Tropical Heat*, a short story that lives up to the "heat" in its name.

If you want to keep in touch, sign up here: http://eepurl.com/hhBhXX

CHAPTER ONE

"Welcome to the Summer of Lizzie. Is everybody ready?" I spread my arms wide as I entered the kitchen, my enthusiasm rivaling a DJ trying to hype up a crowd on a Saturday night. Or so I assumed since I was not the type to go to events with a DJ. "I know I am. I've got on shorts, my new favorite T-shirt—it's super soft—and best of all, my flip-flops!"

I stuck out a foot as proof, and Sarah tilted her head in what I assumed was amusement, gripping a coffee mug like her life depended on its magical elixir. "You're high-energy this morning. But I do love the Winnie the Pooh T-shirt."

I gripped the bottom of the gray heather shirt, which read: *You're braver than you believe*. It had Winnie holding Piglet's hand, with a rainbow arching over them. Each letter in *braver* corresponded with a color in the rainbow. "I've decided the world needs more rainbows."

"You're certainly doing your part." Sarah closed her eyes as she drank in a long swig of coffee. She was dressed in black cotton capris and a plain white T-shirt. In other words, the very opposite of a rainbow.

"Too bad we don't have six kids," I mused. "That way each one could always wear an assigned color, and then we'd truly have a rainbow coalition." I laughed, picturing what a sight that would be. "Keeping them in the proper order would be a nightmare."

"Sure, that's the only flaw in your plan." She took another fortifying sip of coffee, as if the thought of six kids, however imaginary, had sapped every ounce of her strength. "Also, there are seven colors in the rainbow. ROYGBIV."

"I never understood why there are two shades of blue. And the thought of seven kids—" I did a full body cringe.

"Indigo is more purplish."

"You're confusing me. Are you saying you wish we had seven kids?"

"No. I'm informing you of a simple fact about the rainbow." Sarah tilted her head when she knew she had me on a technicality.

Think fast, Lizzie.

"The Pride flag only has six colors. I'm using that as my reference point." I stuck out my tongue at Sarah.

"That's not important, though. Back to the Summer of Lizzie."

"Dare I ask what the Summer of Lizzie is?" Sarah took another glug of coffee.

"Unlike you, who apparently had the time of your life going back to teaching at that fancy charter school of yours, I had a terrible year. I've had a countdown to the first day of summer going on my phone since before Christmas. And, it's here!" I actually attempted a twirl but had to pull up short as a sharp pain sent me reaching for my neck. "This knot is going to be the death of me."

"Still? You need to do something about it."

"I did." I crossed my arms in response to my wife's scolding, flinching as this small act of defiance sent a fresh jolt through my stiff tendons.

"Inga doesn't count."

Up until earlier that week, Inga had been our au pair. Our third au pair, that is, in less than a year. The first one, Valentina, had gotten homesick and left after a month. The second, Sophia, had dumped us for the chance to work for a plastic surgeon's family and travel with them on a private jet to their second house in Beverly Hills. But Inga had been a godsend. Not only had she been great with the kids, she was a whiz when it came to neck massages.

"Inga was almost a professional. Her mother was a genuine Swedish massage instructor, from Sweden, even. I'm really going to miss her. Is the new au pair

3

from Sweden?" I looked hopefully at Sarah, who was only about halfway caffeinated from what I could tell, meaning I had the upper hand in the conversation. Once her needle hit the full line, I'd be three steps behind.

"Eloise is from France. And she doesn't arrive until the end of August."

"I'll be fine until then," I said as I dug my fingertips into my *hard as a rock* neck meat. "Is there such a thing as French massage? You know, like French kissing?"

Sarah blinked. A lot.

I replayed what I had said through my head and realized fairly quickly where I'd gone wrong. "I didn't mean it that way. I just thought, there's Swedish massage. And I know there's French kissing. So I guess I figured if you sort of, you know—" I made a mushing motion with my hand.

"You figured if you somehow combined these two totally unrelated things, you'd end up with a cure for your stiff neck?" The flash of humor in Sarah's eyes told me I had under a minute left before her brain became fully engaged, and she left me in the dust.

"I mean, if that did happen to be the case, sign me up. Only with you, of course." I offered her a saucy wink, but the pitter-patter of kids zipping down the stairwell put an end to the conversation.

Saved by the bell.

Normally, I would have welcomed the opportunity to

flirt with Sarah. After the rough patch we'd experienced with our sex life the previous year, I'd been doing my best to make sure we didn't lose that connection again. I'd even created a recurring reminder in my phone for "Hubba bubba with Sarah" to keep me on task. It was set for every nine days, chosen specifically as a way to make it feel more spontaneous by never being on the same day of the week twice in a row. In fact, the alarm was due to go off later today, if memory served. Flirtatious banter would definitely help my cause, but in the present situation, I wasn't sure how I could extricate myself from my French massage suggestion without causing a massive blunder. My specialty.

Once all four kids—not a single one of them wearing rainbows, by the way—burst into the kitchen, the decibel level reached ear-piercing.

"Where's Inga? I want to go to the park." Olivia asked Sarah, a habit all the kids had. If they needed an answer, I was second choice at best.

"Inga went back home. Remember?" Sarah said softly.

Ollie's face fell. "But it's summer. Lots of park time."

"That's true." I stepped into the fray. "It's the Summer of Lizzie. Do all of you know what that means?"

Olivia and Sarah stared at me like I'd lost my mind. It was a look I was more than a little familiar with, and

I carried on with an explanation as if it hadn't registered.

"It means we're going to have fun every single day to make up for the past two miserable semesters I've had to endure. College kids these days do not want to work at anything, not to mention how politicized the Naz—"

"No politics before toast." Sarah cut me off before I could go on a Nazi tirade. Not for the first time. It was hard to be an early twentieth century German history professor during these interesting times.

"Toast. I can make that."

Sarah didn't fight me on it, but Ollie seemed disappointed I'd put myself in charge of the project. Granted, my track record in the kitchen was dismal at best, but how hard could toast be?

I slotted four pieces of bread into the toaster and pressed the button. "After breakfast, I can take you guys to the park if you'd like."

"Actually," Sarah placed a hand on my shoulder. "We're going to your dad's to swim."

My heart sank. I should've known from the reassuring hand that I wouldn't like the news. It had been over a year since he and Helen, my stepmother, had moved to Massachusetts, but I still hadn't gotten used to seeing him as much as we did. Nearly forty years of parental neglect will do that. It was hard to trust he was truly as reformed a man as he appeared to be, and I was always waiting for the drop of that other shoe, guillotine style. Not literally. He wasn't a monster, but it would hurt because whenever I started to believe in something, it'd be crushed by the universe in some epic fashion.

"Swimming!" the kids chanted, oblivious to my change in mood.

"Right." I clenched my jaw, covering the action by turning it into a smile as best as I could manage. "I keep forgetting he has a pool. How nice."

The bread popped up, and I reached for the first piece, but the moment I made a move, something in my neck snapped, sending a shooting pain throughout my body.

"Fuck!" My hand flew to my neck, though I probably should have clamped it over my mouth, instead. I prayed none of the kids, or Sarah, had heard the F-bomb. Perhaps on account of me being an atheist, God chose not to answer this prayer.

"Fuck! Fuck! Fuck!" Calvin grinned at me, like he knew I couldn't admonish him because I'd said it first.

Sarah threw me some serious shade.

"My neck. It popped." My fingers worked on the spot, and I couldn't tell if it helped or inflicted more pain, but I forged on.

"See a chiropractor, please. Or a massage therapist."

"I hate doctors."

"I hate getting notes from the kids' teachers saying one of them was swearing like a pirate." The singsong way she admonished me made my skin go clammy. It was downright weird, and a little creepy, for her to keep her cool like that, all the while definitely wanting to wring my poor, damaged neck.

"Did pirates use the F-bomb? It doesn't sound very pirate-like to me. If my neck didn't hurt so bad, I'd google it." I made a mental note to research this later.

Sarah spooned blueberries into small bowls, one for each of us. "How's that toast coming along?"

I carefully removed the four pieces, adding another four. "You know what sucks? I don't get worker's comp for this injury."

There was a loud sigh. The type that said not to press the issue and just work through the pain.

After I buttered the first batch, but before the second finished, I popped two Advils, chasing the pills with extra cold water.

By the time we sat for breakfast, my neck was locked up tight. Just as I eased myself into my chair, my *sex with Sarah* phone alarm went off, right on schedule. Not that I usually launched into seduction at the breakfast table, but I found it helpful to have most of the day to mentally prepare for the evening. I don't like surprises, especially the kind that involve being naked. Unfortunately, I was going to need a limber neck to do things right. With a smidgen of guilt, I marked the task done, telling myself I would make up for it when I had complete use of my body again. Whenever that might be.

"Here's to the Summer of Lizzie!" I raised my orange juice glass, refusing to allow myself to be beat by a minor setback.

No one reciprocated.

"Why isn't it the Summer of the Petries?" Sarah shifted in her chair, sending out a vibe I couldn't quite decipher but sensed wasn't good.

"It is. That's what I said." Why was I getting in trouble this time?

"No, you keep saying Lizzie. There are six of us." Her eyes bounced off Freddie and Olivia, our twins, Demi, and our youngest, Calvin.

"You're right! There *are* six of us." I nearly bounded out of my chair with excitement as the number clicked but thought better of it, wondering how much damage that'd do to my neck.

"Did you just figure that out?"

"Yes—no. I mean, I just figured out we can all wear a color of the rainbow without needing any more kids. Why didn't I think of that earlier? Kids, what color of the rainbow would you like to be."

"Blue." Freddie nibbled on a piece of toast.

"Blue." Olivia guzzled her orange juice.

Dang, did that mean indigo was back into the equation, and I now needed a seventh family member for my rainbow coalition? Who would I want around all the time for my plan to work? Did Ghandhi count?

"Blue." Demi kicked her feet under the table, whacking me in the knee.

9

At least I didn't need to figure out who'd be indigo now, since the kids weren't playing rainbow ball.

"Black." Calvin tossed a blueberry into his mouth. Of course, the little rebel opted for the one that was the absence of color.

"Looks like it's going to be the Summer of Bruises," Sarah quipped.

I was about to ask her how she'd gotten to that conclusion, but then I put black and blue together and figured it out on my own, which was no small feat now that Sarah was functioning on all cylinders. As if to reinforce Sarah's prophecy, Calvin threw a blueberry at Freddie, who giggled before reciprocating.

"Boys, do not throw your food!" I moved the bowl out of Calvin's reach. "Calvin, you can't go to school in the fall if you start food fights."

"Can to!" He crossed his tiny arms over his chest. "I'm going to school with Fred."

"To the same school as Fred," I corrected for at least the tenth time. Calvin had it in his stubborn mind he would be with Fred in the same class, no matter how often we explained reality to the boy.

"Freddie and I will be together all the time." He tightened his arms, the look of determination on his little face rivaling some of my own stubborn moments. Was that a trait that was learned, not inherited, since we used Sarah's egg for Calvin?

"At the same school." I dug in, much to Sarah's annoyance based on the grim look on her face.

"You two are in different grades, Cal," Sarah said softly. "We've gone over this before."

"No. I want to be in the same grade!" Calvin shook his tiny head furiously, almost toppling off his chair.

"You and Demi will be in the same grade." Sarah gave Calvin's shoulder a squeeze.

"And, Fred. I want to be with Fred."

"Honey," Sarah leaned forward. "That's not how school works. You can't simply skip grades to be with your big brother. No matter how much you hope for it. You have to start off in kindergarten and work your way up, just like Fred did."

"Then I won't go!" Calvin stormed from the table, shouting on his way out, "I hate school!"

"Can I have his toast?" Ollie asked, unperturbed.

"You can have one of mine." I gave Ollie a slice, my stomach tightening, along with the knot in my neck.

There was a slam of a door on the second level.

"How's the Summer of Lizzie going so far?" There was a glint of teasing humor in Sarah's eyes.

"Don't start." I held up a hand as if to ward off any more threats to my first perfect summer day. "Things are always rocky in the mornings around here, but once we get going, nothing's going to stop us from having the best summer ever. Right kids?"

There was dead silence.

CHAPTER TWO

"Where are my goggles?" Calvin demanded as soon as he got out of the SUV in my dad's curved driveway.

"Where did you leave them?" I responded, knowing it was foolish to ask. Not that I didn't think it important to teach kids to keep track of their own shit, but with four kids under the age of eight, it was an uphill battle just to leave the house to go swimming.

"Here," Sarah chimed in, holding out a straw beach bag big enough to fit supplies for the entire family for a week. "Everything you need is here. For all of you. Now let's get everyone in the pool, including you, Lizzie."

"Head first?" I joked, but given Olivia's evil giggle, I feared I'd regret it.

"You made it." My dad's second wife, Helen, stepped outside, a flowing wrap draped elegantly over her swimsuit. Paired with oversize sunglasses and a turban on her head, she gave the appearance of a classic Hollywood star.

As I glanced to my side, I couldn't help noticing how Sarah also looked impeccable in her one-piece bathing suit and shorts. Between the two of them, I might have wandered into a photoshoot for a magazine dedicated to gracious living. Meanwhile, I sported my usual T-shirt and shorts, making me suddenly feel like some sort of vagabond who had wandered onto the scene uninvited.

I hadn't ever been the type to give a crap about clothes, but for some reason, my deficiencies in this department hit me hard today. Maybe because I couldn't even make toast without suffering bodily injury. I felt frumpy and old.

Unless... could the neck issue be something other than age? Like an illness? My mom had died of cancer. Was there a cancer that made one have a decrepit neck? If I had cancer, I could hardly be expected to dress well, and no one would dare call me frumpy for it. I wasn't sure whether to feel relieved to be let off the metaphorical hook or terrified at the possibility of dying from neck cancer.

We tramped through the kitchen on the way to the pool, a straggly line of fidgety kids that no military commander would ever tolerate. Not that I fancied myself a general, but sometimes I did wish I had a whistle to keep everyone in line. Sadly, Sarah continually put the kibosh on this brilliant idea.

"Finally!" Maddie, who was already sprawled out on a chaise lounge in the sun, lowered her sunglasses. "We didn't think all of you would make it."

"We had a minor disagreement." I didn't name names, but I placed a hand on top of Calvin's head to hint at the culprit. Cal had spent an hour at home refusing to change into his swim trunks unless we agreed he could be in the same grade as Fred.

"I'm not going to school." Calvin shook off my hand and stripped his shirt over his head before cannonballing into the pool, splashing Maddie in the process.

So far, the summer was off to a bumpy start, and something told me, it was only going to get worse. Not wanting to project this, I changed the subject. "Where's Willow?"

"Inside, talking with your dad."

"About?"

Maddie shrugged, recovering her eyes with her glasses and placing her hands over her head. I envied her ability to relax so completely. Even before kids, I'd never mastered this.

"Gramps!"

I jumped at Freddie's outburst, turning to watch him zip toward my father, who had just emerged with Willow from the sliding door onto the deck. He wore palm tree shorts, a white wife beater, and stars and stripes flip-flops. In other words, I had inherited my fashion sense directly from him. Growing up, I'd only seen my father in a three-piece suit. Apparently, retirement made him a lot more easygoing by a factor of a million.

"Lizzie." My father gave me a hug, another thing I'd never experienced in childhood. "The boys have been talking my ear off for days now about some kind of wolf place. Should we take them to play?"

"With wolves?" It was funny because part of me always thought if wolves had raised me, I would have turned out better than having the scotch-lady as my mom.

"No, silly." Willow laughed. "It's a water park."

"For wolves?" I knew something wasn't computing in my brain, but I couldn't figure out where I was going wrong. I seemed to be the only person who didn't understand what was going on, but that wasn't exactly an unusual experience for me.

"Wolf is only in the name. It has nothing to do with wolves." Willow squirted sunscreen onto her palm, smearing it on her left arm before she shook the bottle at Maddie.

"Oh." I'll admit, this was a letdown.

"Don't sound so disappointed." Maddie tsked at me like I was the demented one.

"Wolves are cool," I argued.

"Not as babysitters." Maddie got to her feet to put sunscreen on Willow's back.

I turned to my dad. "I like wolves, even if it is only part of the name. I think we should take all the kids. Are we doing it today?"

"You have to make reservations," my father explained. "It's a family resort thing."

Sarah, whom I didn't know was standing so close to me, chimed in, "That sounds wonderful. I'm looking for ideas for one month from now."

That sounded very specific, and an alarm bell went off in my head, but my father said something that stopped the warning before it could fully materialize.

"Leave it with me. I'll book it for the family."

My father was going to make a reservation at a family resort. Not have his assistant, who no longer worked for him, do it. I was speechless. I was still adjusting to my father not having a driver either, and seeing him behind the wheel gave me the willies. Now this.

Even though my father had moved to Massachusetts well over a year ago, it still took my breath away on occasions when we had what I assumed was normal talk about family time. Perhaps because I had very little experience on that front growing up. For my entire childhood, no one in my family—my dad, brother, or mom—paid me any attention.

In my father's defense, he basically ignored both me and my brother, so it wasn't like I was singled out. He'd been a man of few words, letting my mom do all the talking. A true shame because that woman never had a kind word to say to me, unless you counted saying *lesbian* with poison daggers meant to hack my heart into shreds, painfully slow for maximum suffering.

Which you definitely shouldn't count, just FYI. She was a very mean woman, and I occasionally still had nightmares starring the scotch-lady.

"Gramps, get in!" Ollie floated by in a flamingo inner tube, wearing purple heart-shaped sunglasses. Even my oldest had more style.

"He's—"

But before I could say my father was too old for the pool, the man proved me wrong by diving in headfirst. He looked more like an Olympic swimmer, not the financial whiz I'd grown up with. When had that happened? Apparently, I was the only adult present who could barely turn her neck to one side.

Soon enough, the entire family was there, including Sarah's mom, Rose, and her much-younger husband, Troy. Not that he was all that young now. I was willing to bet, though, he could probably turn his head in both directions without crying, so he had me beat.

Sitting in a chair under an umbrella, I watched my family having the time of their lives in the pool.

Why are you just watching? asked a voice in my head. *Join them, you moron!*

If Mr. Financial Times could lighten up, I could as well.

I called Calvin over. "Shall we surprise Mommy and the grandmas?" I pointed to Sarah, standing in the pool, with her arms on the edge, chatting with Rose and Helen sitting in chairs.

"How?" His eyes grew three times larger.

"Jump in right next to them."

He started to run off, but I stopped him.

"No, together. Let's jump in together."

Halfway through the air, as my neck muscles screamed in protest, I realized my error in thinking this was a good idea. I entered the water, flailing and wondering where I could buy a neck brace on the ride home.

CHAPTER THREE

Adjusting the brace on my neck, I eyed Sarah as she made her way into the library. I wasn't sure what she wanted, unless it was to tell me once again that my neck brace was overkill, and I looked like someone in an old sitcom trying to get away with an insurance scam.

Even if it wasn't that, in all probability, she was there to tell me something I didn't want to know. That seemed to be ninety percent of our conversations lately. Ollie got in trouble at school because she pushed another kid. Fred got a C on a math test because it seems he inherited my numbers skills. Demi glued her fingers together. Calvin won't get in the car. It never ended.

"I don't understand scissoring." Even as the words flew from my mouth, I had no idea where they'd come from or why they had chosen this moment to make their escape.

Sarah didn't break her stride, but by the time she reached my desk, her mouth flapped open like a goldfish trying to get a breath, before she was able to compose herself. "You mean you don't know how to use scissors."

It was difficult to tell if she was asking or stating a fact. Either scenario annoyed me. I mean, I was a grown adult. Just because I wasn't the arts and crafts type, didn't mean I couldn't operate scissors. I wasn't a moron, for fuck's sake.

"Of course, I can use scissors." My tone was much too testy, but I attributed it to my injury. The only thing more annoying than being in pain was having a wife who refused to acknowledge the depths of my suffering.

"Are you sure about that?" This was definitely a question, asked in the way that implied she knew the answer, and I was wrong.

"What do you want me to do to prove it?" I opened my desk drawer, seeking a pair but not finding any because why would I need scissors? That didn't stop me from saying, "Should I cut a circle to prove it to you, like kids have to do in kindergarten?"

"I'm not sure I want you near scissors. You're already maimed enough as it is." She acknowledged my neck brace with an uplifted eyebrow and a bit more mocking than I'd been expecting.

"You're in luck. I can't find a pair." I slammed the desk drawer closed. "It doesn't matter. I wasn't talking about scissors, but scissoring." I boosted my eyebrows to emphasize I meant the sexual act. "I can't picture it."

Sarah's eyes sparkled with realization. "What have you been watching in here?"

"Documentaries."

"Is that Lizzie code for porn?" She playfully crossed her arms, appraising me with a satisfied smirk. "Just because they have real people in them doesn't make them documentaries, you know."

"Are you kidding me? I've never watched porn."

"Oh, I know that. But maybe you should. It might help with the visuals for scissoring." Sarah used her hands to show me how it worked.

What did she mean by *Oh, I know*? How did she know? And did this imply something about my skills in the bedroom? Granted, I'd dismissed my most recent reminder for sex without actually following through, but that wasn't my fault. I was injured!

The fact that she hadn't pushed back even a little on my never having seen porn irked me. Not that I ever had watched porn, but was it that farfetched to believe that I might on occasion? Because I totally could, if I wanted to. I didn't want to. But maybe I should anyway, just to prove all the naysayers wrong. Did they sell T-shirts that proclaimed *I'm a porn watcher*?

I rolled my eyes at Sarah's hand demonstration. "I know the mechanics. But how does it feel good? And, how much stretching does it take beforehand? Because it doesn't seem like an easy thing to do without some sort of elaborate warm-up."

"I really love how your mind works." Sarah's shoulders shook with laughter. "I mean, it terrifies me, too, but…"

"Should we try it?" I acted it out with my own hands, trying to put my finger—so to speak—on what the appeal might be.

Sarah's goldfish face returned, and this time, words seemed to fail her.

"I mean—never mind." I, for one, didn't want to try it, but I was still annoyed by her steadfast belief I wasn't the porn type. Which I'm not, just to be clear. And, I couldn't quite figure out why Sarah already knowing this piece of information bothered me. "Why'd you come in here anyway? What did one of the kids do now?"

"Nothing that I know of, but why did I come in here?" She held onto her nostril for some weird reason. Did a lack of oxygen spur memories? "Oh, right. Ethan and his family are coming for a visit this July."

"Why are they coming to Massachusetts in July? It's miserable here. The heat and humidity. Too many Massholes behind the wheel. Don't even think of taking the train in Boston on Red Sox days. I can't think of any good reason for coming here."

Actually, I could think of many reasons. The mouth-watering scent of hot dogs on the grill. The smell of cut grass. The kids laughing and playing outside. Swimming at my dad's, like we had done earlier in the day. No school for the kids, Sarah, or me. The summer held endless possibilities, and I hadn't given up on the Summer of Lizzie. Sure, the neck brace was a bad start, but it was only day one. Plenty of time to right the summer ship.

The one thing I wasn't looking forward to one iota this July was my birthday. Not simply because I had slipped when talking with my father, letting him know about the five-year plans I'd started when I was ten. This is where I would decide whether or not it was worth continuing to live. If I said yes, I had to stick around for the next five years, no exceptions. I'd found it reassuring, life-affirming, in a way. But I was well aware most people would not see it that way. So many liked to focus on the bad parts.

Anyway, I'd stopped my five-year plans when I met Sarah. She was stuck with me for as long as my body decided to keep ticking, whether she liked it or not. Unless she snapped and offed me. Sometimes, I believed this was only a matter of time. I'd seen enough *Dateline* episodes to know of this possibility. The saving grace was Sarah had her own trust fund and wouldn't do it to get mine.

Where was I? Right. It wasn't really those old five-year plans that were causing me distress, though. It was the fact this year I would be turning forty, and I simply couldn't handle that thought. How was I on the cusp of middle age? It was like one day I was young and the next, not young. Seriously. Life sucked sometimes. Not bad enough to start considering five-year plans again, but—

"Earth to Lizzie!" Sarah shouted through her cupped hands, startling the crap out of me.

"Are you trying to give me a heart attack?" I massaged my galloping heart. Maybe I should make an appointment with a doctor. Get levels for things. When would I have to start getting mammograms? Should I have a dermatologist track all my moles? My mom had died of colon cancer. Was it time for a colon check? My mind whirred with all the things I needed to do.

There was nothing fun about turning forty as far as I could tell.

"Are you back?" Sarah slanted her head to meet my eyes.

"Yes, and I'm also deaf." I shook a finger in my ear. Another appointment I should make.

"Poor baby. So, back to Ethan. Do you think all of them can fit in the apartment over the garage?"

"The three of them?"

"Four, actually."

"Ethan, Lisa, and Casey." I held up three fingers,

completely baffled. Even I couldn't screw up counting to three.

"And Delores." Sarah displayed four.

"Does that mean Ethan and Lisa finally got divorced, and now Lisa and Delores have tied the knot?"

"No and no. But she's coming, and I'm not sure what to call her. Lisa's girlfriend, maybe." Sarah's brow crinkled with confusion. "Are they a throuple?"

I was just as confused as she was. Lisa and Ethan had been married for years, but Ethan wasn't the type who liked sex. Not just weird stuff like scissoring, but any aspect of it. Lisa fell in love with Delores, but didn't want to end the marriage with Ethan because they'd adopted Casey together. Nothing about the Ethan, Lisa, and Delores situation made sense to me, but it wasn't any of my business, really. All I could offer was lifting one shoulder.

"Did you think Lisa and Delores would last this long living with Ethan in our house in Fort Collins?" I had put the odds closer to four months, tops.

"Who's to say what works for other people?" Sarah shrugged it off. "The question is, can they fit into the apartment?"

"That's for the au pair." My spine stiffened.

"Inga's gone, and Eloise isn't arriving until August."

"Even so, that space is reserved. It doesn't seem right to have other people stay there." This wasn't my only concern. The truth was I didn't want to mention I had plans for the space this summer. I never got alone time in the house anymore, and what I really wanted was a place to put together my jigsaw puzzles while listening to audiobooks in peace. Last summer, I'd tried constructing a bunker, but those plans had been sadly destroyed after Rose had gotten it into her head it was a sex bunker. To be clear, it wasn't that Rose was disgusted. She was jazzed about the idea, which pretty much killed it for me.

Dear God, did Rose know more about scissoring than I did?

I jabbed my eyes with my fingers, erasing that visual.

"All the bedrooms are full, and Maddie and Willow live in the basement," Sarah argued with a reasonableness that drove me stark raving mad. "We don't have anywhere else to put them."

"My dad's house has five bedrooms and nine bathrooms. Surely, they can bunk there." See? I could be reasonable, too.

"They're driving out here—"

"They're driving from Fort Collins to Wellesley?" I slammed my palms on my desk, leaning forward. "Has Ethan lost his mind?"

Sarah shrugged. "Casey's developed a fear of flying."

"Really?" That shocked the hell out of me because Casey was razor sharp. In fact, she was who I'd tasked with figuring out a way of moving us to Mars because the earth was beyond fucked. Fear of flying added a troublesome wrinkle to that plan.

"I think the apartment will work." Sarah's tone implied the matter was settled.

"It only has a queen-sized bed," I argued anyway.

"The couch pulls out. Two can sleep on it."

"But there are three adults."

"They can work that part out." There was no doubt Sarah's mind was made up, and even I had to admit defeat occasionally.

"How long will they be here?" I asked with an ill-concealed sigh. Just because I was giving in didn't mean I had to pretend to be happy about it.

"A week."

I nodded. One week. That wasn't too bad, giving me plenty of puzzle time. "When in July will they be here?"

"They'll arrive on the thirteenth."

My suspicions flared. That was the day before my birthday. My *fortieth* birthday.

"Why that day?"

"They chose it." Sarah shrugged, leaving the office.

"Did you tell them to arrive on that day?" I yelled at her retreating back, but she didn't break her stride.

As far as I knew, Sarah wasn't planning a birthday party for me, and I had recently told her not to, or I'd divorce her. I didn't supply my reasons for why. Not that I had to. She probably assumed, with me being the people-hater, I didn't want a big fuss.

And she was right, but it went even deeper than that.

The last thing I wanted to do was to ring in my midlife years with all my friends and family to witness it. I didn't know why, but reaching forty seemed like a total failure on my part. Ironic, given at the age of ten I had instituted my five-year plans and surely never expected to make it so far. You would think reaching forty would be something to celebrate with my family —another thing I never thought I'd have, or at least not one that loved me.

But I dreaded being old.

I didn't want to wear a neck brace every time I had a twinge, even if Sarah did think I put it on for the attention. I didn't want to say I never watched porn and have people believe me without a hint of questioning. I didn't want to be considered a stick in the mud, even if that was the way most people would describe me. Including myself, if I had to be honest.

What could I do to dispel this fun-hating image? I'd jumped into the pool with Calvin, and lived to regret it. I massaged my neck, which hadn't forgiven me. Whatever I needed to do to not be considered over-the-hill, I feared it was going to take a hell of a lot more effort on my part to achieve.

CHAPTER FOUR

"You think I'm a stick in the mud, don't you?" I accused Sarah when she came to bed later that night. It was possible I hadn't been able to get that thought out of my head since the scissoring convo. I'd taken off my neck brace and been pleased to find I could turn my head nearly half the usual distance, but this did nothing to lessen the sting of being thought dull.

"Is that your way of telling me I'm not getting any tonight?" Sarah climbed under the covers. "I'm too exhausted to even try to talk you into any nookie. Not even naked cuddling."

"Do you not find me attractive anymore? I'm getting older, so I can kinda see why and wouldn't blame you." I patted my stomach, which I'd been obsessing about for several hours now. It seemed that overnight it had doubled in size. "Since the kids, I don't go on my bike rides like I used to. It seems I never have enough hours in the day to do all the things."

Sarah rolled onto her side, placing a hand on my cheek. "Don't ever think that. Ever. I find you as attractive now as I did when we first met."

"I was wearing a sweater vest that day. I think that's another tick in the fuddy-duddy column, don't you? Along with getting older and wider." I pulled the covers higher, all the way to my tits, which were getting bigger as well. Sadly, after decades of being no-shows, they'd arrived just in time to start sagging. It didn't seem fair. I'd had to learn to live without tits in my twenties, when I could've really used them, only to get them right in time for middle age.

"Not sure how to break this to you, but I'm also getting older, and after being pregnant twice, my body has changed significantly."

"True, but you look amazing all the damn time. Besides, it's not fair that I'll always reach all of our age milestones before you." Like turning forty, not that I could bear to put that into words and speak them out loud. "It's not nice."

"Not nice?" She chuckled quietly. "You're acting like it's my fault. I can't go back in time and be born before you. Sometimes you have to accept life can be brutal."

"How about we go away for a weekend?" I was

both surprised by and proud of my spontaneous exclamation.

"What?" Sarah yawned, hippopotamus style, giving me a good look at all her teeth. Clearly, she was not as impressed by me as I was.

"A weekend away, just the two of us. We could get your mom to watch the kids." It was a stroke of genius on my part. Not only would I get points for planning something romantic, if I played my cards right, we could have sex twice on the trip so I could make up for marking my reminder done the other day when that hadn't been the case. Total win-win.

"Mm, okay," Sarah mumbled into her pillow.

It only took four minutes for Sarah to start snoring softly. Given I now had two weeks' notice, there was plenty of time to figure out a way to rock her world. Just not with scissoring, because I would never be limber enough for that.

I cranked my neck to the right and then left, the twinge still definitely there.

I needed to convince Sarah I wasn't a stick in the mud in any part of life. Sure, I had moves more like Herman Munster with my stiff neck, but there had to be something I could do about it.

Not wanting to make a doctor's appointment—I hated them—I pulled out my phone and looked up massagers on Amazon. It was difficult to get freaky in bed when you couldn't move.

Funny how much I'd changed. *Before Kids Lizzie* rode

a bike every day. Shaved all my parts, not just my legs and pits. Never wore day-old clothes. Was fastidious.

I rubbed my legs together under the sheets, trying to determine if it had been four or five days since the last time I ran a razor over them.

No wonder Sarah would rather sleep. Did everyone at the pool get a chuckle over my stubble? Every other woman there had managed to look like she'd stepped out of a magazine, but not me. Not by a long shot. I was bent over like Quasimodo. I needed to do something about that, at least, even if a total makeover wasn't in my future.

I scrolled through several shiatsu options on my screen that looked a little too intense. I noticed an option for handheld devices, which seemed more my speed. But as soon as I clicked on it, my eyes boggled as Amazon recommended a selection of items that were a bit too phallic in shape to be regular massage devices.

Suddenly, I was shopping for vibrators.

How had this happened? I slid my eyes toward the smart speaker on Sarah's bedside table. Had the powers that be been listening to our conversation and decided a vibrator was just what was needed for our weekend away?

They might not be wrong.

Anyway, it wouldn't hurt to peruse the options. Aside from getting my neck back to working order, my main goal for the summer was to up my bedroom game. There was nothing fuddy-duddy about a vibrator. That was for certain.

There was one that was small—I'd always been kinda terrified of the larger ones, unsure really what to do with them. Smaller was better. It wasn't expensive by any means, and it came in pink. That color didn't scare me one bit. In fact, it was one of my favorite shades despite no one actually believing me when I said this. Apparently, my demeanor didn't really scream pink. I also love the singer P!nk, but that was an entirely different subject, and I wasn't sure how my brain made that leap.

Now that I did have P!nk—the singer—in my head, I put my ear buds in to listen to P!nk's rendition of "I Touch Myself," which I was sorely tempted to do.

Sarah rolled over, her hand slapping my phone out of my grip. How, in her sleep, did the woman know I was contemplating being naughty? Not that I would. I didn't want to end up in traction.

Gently, I moved Sarah's arm back to her side of the bed and picked up my phone. Instead of overthinking it, my specialty, I purchased the vibrator. For us. I wanted to surprise her during our weekend away.

CHAPTER FIVE

The one thing I did not consider when ordering a surprise vibrator for my wife is that since it came from our joint account, the default address contained both our names. I thought I had changed it to just me, but the more I tried to remember, the less certain I became. This would have been no big deal, except Sarah had elevated intercepting and opening Amazon packages I preferred for her not to see to an Olympic sport.

This is why, on the day I anticipated the package arriving, I was checking my phone every fifteen minutes. Finally, I saw that the Amazon delivery person was a few blocks away. I slipped on my flip-flops, my hand on the front doorknob.

"Where are you going?" Sarah seemed to appear out of nowhere, scaring the crap out of me. I swear she was a witch in a former life.

"For a walk with Gandhi." This much was true, but my main goal was to cut off the delivery guy before anyone in our household spied the package.

"Can you take Freddie and Calvin with you? They're driving me bonkers." Sarah didn't wait for an answer, kissing my cheek as she passed by, like that was going to make me feel better.

Having the kids in tow would complicate my mission, and I had to wonder if Sarah knew I was up to something. It was nearly impossible to get anything past the woman. That didn't stop me from trying, but each time I failed, it dented my ego, even while reinforcing my stubborn desire to try again.

"Boys!" I called out. "Time for a walk."

Olivia rushed to the door, putting a hand on her hip. "Just the boys? That's dis-crim-nation."

"Did you want to come with us? The more the merrier." My brain kicked into hyper drive. If Freddie held onto Gandhi's leash, I might have time to stash the package into a bush without any of the kids witnessing the act.

Maybe I was overreacting. It wasn't unusual for us to receive packages, after all. And in all likelihood, even if someone found it and brought it in, it would sit on the counter unopened until one of us had space to breathe. With four kids, plus Maddie and Willow living in our basement, and countless pop-ins by family, we didn't get a lot of downtime. If only Sarah didn't have that uncanny sixth sense when it came to busting me in the middle of doing something shady and/or stupid. To be fair, I engaged in such activities pretty regularly.

Even as I planned and plotted, I knew deep down this would be the one time Sarah would open the box immediately, ruining the vibrator surprise. Unless... What if something worse happened? What if someone like my dad opened the box? He'd never done so in the past, but one thing I've learned in all my years is I had rotten luck. The one and only time I'd ordered a sex toy in my life, my father would magically descend from a rope in the sky and immediately find it.

"I wanna go, too." Demi rushed to put her shoes on.

"Looks like all the kids are going with me," I called out to Sarah.

She strutted into the entryway, an odd smile on her face. "I'm expecting a delivery. Which one of you is going to bring it inside for Mommy?"

All four kids raised their hands. I was in some serious trouble now.

"What delivery? I didn't know we were expecting anything." If Sarah hadn't suspected I was up to something before, the way my voice cracked not once, but at least four times, more than likely put her on high alert.

"Perhaps it's a surprise." There was a saucy wink.

Fuck.

Had she checked our orders and knew what was

coming? I should have created a different account to order it or had it shipped somewhere private. This was why I needed a bunker!

"What is it?" I should have left it alone, but after nearly four decades, I still didn't possess enough self-preservation.

"If I tell you, it won't be a surprise, now will it?"

"A surprise for whom?" My eyes bounced off each child, Sarah's face not giving the game away.

After a very long second, wearing a cryptic expression, Sarah answered, "Maybe it's for me."

Sometimes I wanted to bop her right on the nose, but what kind of example would that set for my children? I was already in the running for worst mother on the planet by taking four kids and a dog on a walk as a ruse to hide a sex toy from my wife. The last thing I needed was to give Sarah's nose a bop and accidentally start a nose bleed. That would be the time those police types came knocking, asking for a donation for their fraternity, and I'd be hauled off to jail for battery.

There was rotten luck, and then there was my type that was fifty levels worse than rotten. I could never discover the right term for it, so I'd started calling it Lizzie's Law.

Outside, I asked, "Fred, wanna hold Gandhi's leash?"

"No. I'm looking for birds." He moved his head to the right and then left. I envied how effortlessly he managed it. My neck was pretty much back to normal now, but I still hadn't forgotten my ordeal.

"Calvin?"

He tucked his hands into his armpits.

Before I could ask Ollie or Demi, the two girls held hands and skipped ahead, singing "Let it Go." I so wish I could.

Now I was definitely stuck with Gandhi, who pulled the leash, making it clear I wouldn't be able to stand back a bit. We turned right when we reached the sidewalk, and to my left, I spotted the delivery van pulling up to my driveway. The man hopped out, setting a big cardboard box on our rock retaining wall near the front entrance and then diving back into the van.

Just how large was this vibrator, anyway? I'd expected something much smaller, and now I was shaking from alarm. Had I ordered the wrong size? One for horny giants?

I could only watch all this happening over my shoulder, helpless to grab the box and squirrel it away. The kids had extra pep in their step, like walking was their favorite form of entertainment today. So far, though, Sarah had not emerged from the house. Maybe she hadn't noticed the delivery. I might still have time.

Except, no.

Before we turned the corner, I helplessly watched Rose pulling into our driveway. Now I was definitely screwed. She was the type who'd notice a package and bring it inside. Living so close to one's mother-in-law presented many challenges, and this day just ticked a new *what the fuck* box.

The palpitations in my chest kicked to heart attack level, reminding me I wasn't a spring chicken anymore. I was almost forty! I could see the headline now. *Woman drops dead because she ordered a horny-giant-sized vibrator for her mother-in-law*. Because it would get twisted that way for the clicks.

"Look, Mommy!" Fred pointed to a tree. "Red cardinal."

"Good job, Freddie!" Didn't red cardinals have something to do with death? This was probably the end. My heart was going to burst, and then I would die, and Sarah would find the vibrator without me ever being able to explain.

Life could be so cruel.

Calvin slowed his roll, walking in time with me.

"What's up, little man?" I patted the top of his head. I didn't want him to worry. Also, it was possible my pulse was slowing, and the whole heart attack thing may have been a false alarm. This time.

"I hate walking." His tiny shoulders folded inward.

"We just found a red cardinal. Isn't that exciting?" Come to think of it, red cardinals were supposed to represent people who were already dead, so I was in the clear.

He shook his head.

"Why'd you come on the walk, then?"

"Mom's p-punishing me." He stumbled a bit, both on a word and on the cracked sidewalk, and I had to stifle my laughter over the timing.

"What'd you do?"

"N-nothing." He crossed his scrawny arms, and it was even more difficult not to laugh at his defiance.

"Mom isn't the type to punish someone willy-nilly." I should know, since I pretty much deserved all the shade Sarah had thrown my way over the years. Just now, her mom was probably opening my vibrator box, and after the debacle of the supposed sex bunker I attempted building last year, this was only going to make things more awkward with Rose.

"She's unfair. I want to be in the same class as Freddie."

"You want to take music lessons?" It was a pathetic attempt to divert his attention, but I was exhausted from this conversation, which had been happening on a loop for what felt like an eternity.

"No. School. The same grade."

I sighed. "It's just not possible."

"Ollie is."

"They're the same age, Cal. Literally, they were born on the same day. You're starting kindergarten this fall with Demi." The pandemic messed up Demi's schooling, but it worked out having both Calvin and Demi in the same grade. Or so I'd thought.

"I want to be with Fred. Demi can be with Ollie."

"I understand and appreciate your logic, but Calvin,

you're younger than Freddie and Ollie. We can't put you into the grade you want. That's up to the school."

"You're a teacher. F-fix it." When angry, he stuttered a bit, something I found adorable but knew better than to say.

"I'd love to, but I don't think my authority will translate to this situation." I hated seeing him so upset, but it was one thing I was learning as a parent. The pain of disappointing childish minds was unavoidable sometimes.

"I hate—" He didn't finish his statement, running ahead to take the lead, not that Fred noticed. He was too busy trying to spy another cardinal.

My heart clenched, but this time I knew it wasn't a myocardial infarction in progress.

Had he been about to say he hated the system... or me?

It didn't escape my notice that my youngest child wanted to be the oldest kid in the family all the while I was freaking out about turning forty. Life was funny that way. None of us was happy and always thought others had it better.

CHAPTER SIX

By some sort of miracle, the package was still on the rock wall when I returned from the walk thirty minutes later with four kids dragging behind me, carrying a worn-out dog in my arms.

"Look! There's Mommy's box!" Fred took off like a shot before I could stop him, racing up the driveway.

"No. Me!" Calvin gave chase, arriving second, and trying to rip the box from Freddie's hands. "Me!"

Even Ghandhi wriggled free from my arms and did his best to give chase before running out of leash.

Where had all of this energy come from? I hadn't a clue. But there was no chance of beating them to the box at this point, so I tried to make the best of it.

"It's okay, boys. You can both carry the box. Teamwork. It's the Petrie way. Or do you want me to take it inside?" It was a shameless attempt at tricking them, made worse because they didn't even fall for it.

Both boys valiantly shook their heads as if bringing in the package would be the greatest service of their entire lives.

To add insult to injury, it took three times longer than it needed to as the boys each held one side of the box, carefully taking a step forward. I could have had it inside and hidden in my bunker by the time they made it to the door. If they'd let me touch it. And if I'd had a bunker. At that moment, my life was filled with so many regrets.

Ollie tossed her hands up in the air and marched around them.

Demi reached for my hand, staring up at me. "Are we getting ice cream?"

"There's an idea. I think we should ask your mom." I might not be able to wrestle the kids to the ground and take the package, but if I distracted them with ice cream, I'd have a fighting chance of sneaking it away.

"I *am* asking my mom." Demi giggled conspiratorially.

"The one in charge," Fred helpfully declared as his arms strained, trying to right the box.

"He has a point. Mom knows the schedule." I gave a *what can you do* shrug.

Now, I was fully aware I should be privy to the family's goings-on since Sarah had made a great effort to put everything on our shared calendar apps on our phones. It was annoying, really. Because I also entered all of my school and work events there, so whenever I peeked at the calendar—and saw every second of my life accounted for—a cold dread spread from my heart to every extremity. So I'd stopped looking, relying completely on reminders to keep me on task and remaining blissfully oblivious to anything else. It was a foolproof system.

"Check out you two working together!" Sarah clapped, looking at me to silently query if the boys had fought.

I motioned so-so with a hand, before bending down to unclasp Gandhi's leash, the dog scuttling toward his dish to slurp water before he'd cuddle up on his bed for a long snooze.

What wouldn't I give to be either our dog or cat? No adulting whatsoever and to have a houseful of people to ensure every need was met before it even became pressing. I wondered where I could sign up. If it turned out there was such a thing as reincarnation, I wanted to make my preferences known.

"Let's open the box!" Sarah seemed way too excited. Something was definitely up.

"What? Why?" I babbled. "Won't that ruin the surprise?"

I'll tell you what would really be a surprise. Opening an innocent looking Amazon box only to discover a vibrating dildo that had clearly been designed for Goliath.

"You can't keep stuff in a box indefinitely," Sarah

pointed out in her most reasonable tone. I really disliked that tone.

"Hello, Lizzie." Rose held an iced coffee.

I tipped my head in her direction, all the while saying to Sarah, "I can."

My brain raced to come up with something, anything, to convince Sarah not to unpack that box right now. Not only were all the kids present, but so was her mother, a woman who already considered me in a new light because of the sex bunker.

Against all reason, that had improved her opinion of me in a way I'd rather not have known. After years of the woman not liking me, now she did, but it was for all the wrong reasons. If she found out I'd somehow ordered the world's largest vibrator, my latest debacle was only going to complicate an already delicate situation.

Sarah ran the blade of our scissors over the packaging tape, lifting one flap and then the other. I wished this was the moment I discovered I was a witch and could *poof* my way out of this world to a safe place in an alternative reality where human embarrassment wasn't a thing. Because I was about to be served the biggest dose of humiliation ever. A life-threatening amount.

But instead of a mammoth-sized sex toy, Sarah pulled out a couple of the protective air pockets and then fished out what looked to be a LEGO set. "Here's the first surprise, kids."

It was a surprise, for sure. What were LEGOs doing in the box with my vibrator?

Oblivious to my confusion, Sarah handed toys all around. There was one for each kid, though Calvin's face fell when his brother got a more advanced Star Wars kit.

"I want Freddie's!" Cal screeched.

I braced for the battle, but Freddie simply handed his OBI-Wan Kenobi's Jedi Starfighter to Calvin, who gave Fred his Clone Troopers.

"Crisis averted," Rose joked, taking another sip of coffee.

The girls seemed happy with their gifts.

Sarah fished in the box. "Aha!"

I tensed. "I think the rest of the order can wait."

With her hand still in the box, Sarah asked, "Why?"

"It's too much." I'd been lulled into a false sense of safety by the toys, but my imminent humiliation still loomed.

"Surprises overwhelm you?" Sarah asked.

"Too many at once do." I rubbed my chest, suddenly aware of how tight it felt.

"I have news for you, this one is for you, and it fits your mood." Sarah unfurled a T-shirt that had two tits, of the bird variety, with *Calm Your Tits* emblazoned over the chest.

"I love it." I grinned, so delighted by the gift that I almost forgot my impending embarrassment.

But instead of pulling out the vibrator, which I had begun to hope was at least normal size based on how many other things were in the big box, Sarah closed the flaps and left it on the kitchen island. Had I escaped all mortification?

"Is that it?" I asked, fearing the answer but unable to trust my good fortune. Lizzie's Law, in fact, demanded the vibrator appear at the last second when my defenses were weak.

"Didn't you get yourself something?" Freddie asked Sarah.

"Not this time."

"Ice cream," Demi suggested as if that was the greatest gift of all. And really, who could argue?

"It's early—" Sarah started, but after staring into Demi's pleading eyes, she caved. "But, it is hot. What does everyone say? Should we go for ice cream?"

Even I darted a hand in the air.

"Did someone say ice cream?" Willow came up the basement stairs with a plastic Amazon bag in her hand. "Lizzie, I forgot this came for you yesterday."

The package was small and, dare I say it, vibrator shaped. Or rather, it looked like it had a rectangle inside that was about the size I was expecting. That had to be it. Apparently, I'd put my own name on it, after all. Not to mention the slow shipping option, which I'd selected in order to gain $2.25 in digital credits, had been upgraded to arrive early. All my worry had been for nothing. The lesson here was to always check my notifications when expecting a sex toy in the mail to avoid giving myself a coronary. We got so many packages it was hard to keep up.

"What'd you get?" Freddie's eyes boggled with hope.

"Uh—something for work. Nothing exciting." I tucked the bag behind my back.

"I want to see." For a kid who didn't speak much his first few years on the planet, Freddie was becoming quite the chatter bug.

"Work schmurk. Let's get ice cream. Right, Demi?" Inwardly, I cringed over using Demi, but the kid loved ice cream. And let's face it. I could use a Hail Mary.

There was a whoop, and everyone forgot all about the bag behind my back.

During the confusion of getting shoes on four pairs of tiny feet, I shoved the vibrator package into the entryway closet.

Perhaps Lizzie's Law was starting to turn?

CHAPTER SEVEN

When I finally had a moment to myself in the library, I opened the plastic bag. It contained a smaller box inside. I'd expected the packaging to be discreet. Instead, there was a full color photo of a life-size vibrator printed on each of the four sides. As I held it in my hands, turning it round and round, I'd never felt more like a total pervert.

Naturally, as I was staring at the photos on the box, trying to work up the courage to open it, the door to the library started to open. I shoved the box into my lap.

"Why do you have the door closed?" Sarah rolled her neck side to side, but she was not wincing in pain. That was a good sign for our upcoming weekend away.

"I was finishing up a Zoom call," I lied. "What's up?"

"Guess who I just spoke to." Sarah took a seat in the chair on the other side of the desk.

I casually let the box fall to my feet, coughing to cover the sound of it landing.

"Are you getting sick?" She leaned forward as if she meant to check my forehead.

Rubbing my chest, I said, "Tickle in my throat."

Sarah took this as fact and repeated, "Guess who I just spoke to."

"Santa, and none of our children are getting gifts." I wasn't sure about the kids, but I was dead certain Santa had me on the *lump of coal* list.

Sarah's face puckered. "That's mean. They're wonderful kids."

"At least eighty-seven percent of the time." I chuckled, waiting for Sarah to argue the point.

"That's higher than I would have said." She held my gaze expectantly, apparently not willing to give up on her guessing game quite yet.

"I have no idea who you talked to," I told her. "Maybe the Easter Bunny."

"You're terrible at this game."

"Considering there are eight billion people on the planet, this *guess who I spoke to* question is absurd."

Sarah let out a grunt, rolling her eyes heavenward in what I assumed was a silent plea. "You're no fun when you're in this mood."

"What mood?"

"Whatever mood you're in." Sarah gave a long,

pained sigh. "Fine. I talked with Janice. She and Bailey are visiting in July."

"I thought Ethan was visiting in July." Janice was a friend from my grad school days, and Bailey, her younger cousin, had started dating my half-brother, Allen. Were they still dating? I thought the pandemic had killed—what a terrible word choice—the mood.

"He is, along with Janice and Bailey."

"Sarah." I leveled dead serious eyes on my wife. "I told you not to plan anything for my birthday. Please stop. Tell everyone to stay home."

"I have no idea why you think this is all about you. Maybe everyone's looking forward to visiting Massachusetts this summer. Even Gabe and Allen."

"My brothers are also coming?" This was news to me and upped my suspicion levels to new heights as Sarah nodded. My heart jumped into my throat, making it difficult to ask what I really wanted to know. Was Peter coming, too?

Sarah didn't seem to notice I was dying inside, so I finally forced out, "Is that everyone?"

"I think so." Sarah seemed perplexed.

"Peter?"

"He's on house arrest," Sarah pointed out.

"But that doesn't mean he didn't ask for special release or something. Did he?" I demanded.

"Not to my knowledge. He loves you, though."

Should I tell her how I was relieved or let her think I was wallowing that my oldest brother didn't want to come out for whatever birthday torture Sarah had in the works? If she thought I was upset, would she make her way around the desk to give me a hug and see the vibrator box at my feet? It'd be hard to miss the packaging.

"I get it," I said quickly. "I imagine it's hard for him with the legal issues. Between his living arrangements and Demi…"

She nodded, her eyes filled with sadness. "I can't imagine what it's like for him. Being away from his only child. He loves all the photos I send. Sometimes I wonder if I'm punishing him, but he always seems happy and asks for more." She got out her phone. "This is the latest one I sent."

It was from when we went for ice cream. All four kids had ice cream smeared around their mouths, and Demi and Calvin had their arms around each other. It was adorable, but that wasn't the point, which I hoped my deep frown conveyed.

"You still send Peter photos?" One worry that kept me up at night was Peter deciding he wanted Demi to live with him again. He'd given up his parental rights before heading to prison, but if he asked, how could we say no? He was her father.

"Of course, I do."

I smothered my mouth to stop myself from asking why she thought that a good idea.

"If I were in his shoes, I'd want them," she replied to my unasked question.

She had a point, because I would as well. That didn't appease the fear swirling inside. Again, though, I wanted to keep her on the other side of the desk. I had to play it cool.

"I didn't know. That's all." I paired this with a nonchalant shrug. In reality, it would take a few days to mull this over to determine how I really felt about it.

"I didn't think you'd approve." Sarah's tone was a mix of relief and suspicion.

"Yet you did it anyway." Of course, she did. Sarah always did what she thought was right. It was a trait I admired, even if, in this particular case, I thought it might backfire spectacularly.

"You don't approve of a lot of things. Not at first."

What would Sarah say if I said there was a vibrator grasped between my feet?

"You're right about that." I squeezed my feet tighter and tucked them deeper beneath my chair. "I worry. That's all."

"Me too, but he is her father."

"She loves it here, though. She has three siblings who adore her. Look at the photo. She's happy. Like really happy."

"I think that's the part Peter likes. To know he made the right choice. It's a decision no parent should have to make, but he did for her sake." Sarah's voice cracked.

I massaged my eyes, getting rid of the tears. "I can't imagine."

"Dinner will be ready soon." Sarah got to her feet. "You're it for dishes."

Normally, I would argue, but I decided not to press my luck. The longer she stayed in the room, the greater the chance of ruining the surprise between my feet.

"It'll be my pleasure."

Sarah stopped in her tracks. "Please, don't worry about Demi and Peter. Everything will work out the way it should."

I bobbed my head, my tight-lip smile speaking volumes.

Without prompting, Sarah closed the door.

Leaning over in my chair, I swept the box into my hand, taking the pink vibrator out of the thin protective packaging material.

"It's smaller than I thought," I said to myself, holding it at eye level.

There was a USB cord with a needle-like thing on the end that had to be inserted into the vibrator. I tried poking the needle into the bottom, not having much success. I failed with the top.

"Where do I poke this thing?"

Lizzie, stop talking to yourself. If Sarah comes in and sees, she'll know you've lost your mind.

I scanned the directions. There was a tiny hole near

the base, and it took some oomph to pierce the device, causing me to wince, like it was alive or something.

Plugging the USB into my computer, I piled a stack of books and notebooks on the device.

It was time for dinner with my family, and I felt like the dirtiest perv on the planet.

CHAPTER EIGHT

"Are you okay with bunk beds?" Sarah, sitting at the kitchen island, tapped a pencil against her chin.

"You don't want to share a bed with me anymore? This isn't for our weekend away, is it?" I grabbed a cold bottle of water from the fridge.

"I was thinking we should rent a lake house when all the guests are in town, but it's slim pickings on last-minute rentals."

"When were you thinking? Tomorrow?"

"No. Soonish."

I was the one who was terrible with numbers, not Sarah. She was intentionally keeping the date to herself. "Please, whatever you're planning, I don't want a birthday party."

She ignored that and asked, "Do you think the kids would be okay in bunk beds?"

"Uh." I squeezed water from the sports bottle into my mouth, thinking. "Do Fred and Ollie get the top bunks? I can't see Demi liking that option. Or, Fred really."

"My guess is Ollie and Calvin."

"Will Calvin get scared, though. I know he's on a mission to prove he's older than the planet, but he is still our baby boy."

Sarah reached for my bottle, taking a drink. Immediately, I crossed the kitchen and got a glass out of the cupboard for her, filling it with cold water from the tap in the fridge.

"You really hate sharing anything, don't you?" she asked.

"Maybe I was trying to be nice by getting you water." The look she gave me said she wasn't buying it, and my shoulders slumped. "Okay, fine. I hate sharing."

"I'm surprised you haven't suggested bunk beds for us."

"I didn't think you'd go for it."

She stared at me, not blinking, as she no doubt contemplated whether or not I was serious. In my defense, I actually hadn't considered it before. Now that I was, I couldn't deny there was a certain appeal to it. As long as I got the bottom bunk. The older I got, the more cautious I became. Besides, there was probably an age limit on bunk beds. I wouldn't be surprised to discover a warning that read: *Not for use by anyone over forty*. Still, the idea was growing on me.

The longer the silence spread out between us, the more I realized I might be in serious trouble.

Finally, I broke. "I was kidding. How would we naked cuddle if we slept in bunk beds?"

"What's n-naked cuddling?" Calvin climbed up on a step stool to reach the chair next to Sarah, splaying his fingers on the countertop, wearing a serious expression like he was presiding over a board meeting.

"It's where you hold your sleeping teddy bear really close." Sarah, quick on her feet with a child-friendly save, patted his head. Calvin pulled away.

"I don't have a teddy bear," he protested.

"That's true. You have a Baby Yoda." The fact that Sarah was holding back a laugh truly impressed me, but not nearly as much as her ability to come up with a plausible explanation on the fly.

"Do you know what bunk beds are?" Sarah asked our youngest.

"Sure."

Sarah didn't seem to believe him because she showed him a photo on her phone. "Would you like to sleep on the top bunk?"

Calvin's soulful eyes boggled with excitement. "Are we getting bunk beds?"

"Not permanently. We're planning a family vacation."

"What's that?"

"That's where we go away together to have fun and relax," Sarah explained.

"Those two words don't quite go together. Not with this family." I swatted a fruit fly away from my nose. It was impossible this time of year not to have at least five of the little buggers causing a nuisance.

"Are you okay?" Sarah eyed me with skepticism.

"I hate fruit flies. How can we obliterate them from the planet? What purpose do they serve, really?"

"They're used in medical labs. We're genetically similar to them, so those studies help humanity." Seriously, Sarah seemed to have an answer for everything.

I crossed my arms. "Are you saying you condone fruit fly torture?"

"You said you wanted to exterminate them."

I blew out a breath, partially in consternation and partially to chase off another of the little pests. "Not for real. If I could figure out a way to escort them from our house without harming them, I would."

"They should join the circus!" Calvin not-so-helpfully suggested, adding, "Like that school. Can I join the circus?"

"What school?" I googled it on my phone, pulling up a Wikipedia page about The Flying Fruit Fly Circus. "It really is a thing in Australia. But it's for kids, not fruit flies."

"I know," Calvin said with the air of a dean at a university. "I want to go."

"It's in Australia, honey. That's on the other side of the world. Meaning it's really far." Sarah used her *don't get disappointed* mom voice.

"What about gymnastics?" I offered, all the while trying not to smash another fruit fly that buzzed around my head, now aware we were related. No, not related. Similar. Even so, it was too close to murder for my taste.

"That's a great idea!" Sarah flashed me an appreciative smile like I'd never had a good idea before. "I'll ask the rest of the Petrie clan who wants to sign up."

"Not it. Once at school, we had to complete an obstacle course, and the last challenge was a somersault. I couldn't figure it out. I kept trying and trying, until one of the teachers told me it was okay. I didn't need to do it." My body tensed from the memory. "I still feel like a failure." It didn't help that my mother shouted taunts from the sidelines. The one time she showed up to an event, and that happened. Lizzie's Law.

"You can't do a somersault?" Calvin was practically gloating. "I can!"

"Let's go outside on the lawn, and you can show me," Sarah said, probably eager to get him out of my direct line of sight until my temper, which had spiked at his teasing, cooled. Before he managed to jump off the high bar stool, Sarah lifted him to the ground, much to Calvin's annoyance. "Go tell your siblings we're having a somersault competition."

Calvin zipped off on his mission.

"What are we going to do with that kid? He wants to be a grown-up before he's even started kindergarten." My heart raced with the prospect of Cal applying for college before he was ten. Not because he was graduating high school early, but to show us he was ready to fly the coop before the rest of the kids.

"Being the baby is hard. He'll be the last one to reach a lot of the milestones."

"He should savor it, because from where I'm standing, being the old lady in the room is the pits."

CHAPTER NINE

In my office, I tried answering a work email, but my focus was on my One-A-Day history calendar.

June 30th.

My birthday was on July 14th, meaning I only had fourteen days until my life entered—no, don't say it.

I stared at the date, not believing it. But as I recalled my neck issues and all the other little aches and pains of late, there was also no denying it. I was on the threshold of middle age.

How did I get here?

Forty. It wasn't a number that sat well with me. Everyone focused on the horror of turning thirty, but I didn't get that. I may have at one point, but now that I was staring at forty—how had it happened so fast?

Sarah's voice rang in my head, not quite clear but definitely her, and I glanced up, not seeing my wife.

Apparently, forty wasn't just about becoming

middle-aged, but it also bordered crazy town. There was something I didn't need. To say I already had a loose grip on reality was an understatement.

I heard Sarah's voice again, muffled and annoyed. Yet she still wasn't in the room.

What was worse? The fact I was getting old or that I was losing my mind?

I googled *early onset dementia*, finding eleven signs that were cause for concern. Scanning through them, my heart thumped louder in my head. I hit print on the document.

Sarah burst into the library. "Why aren't you answering me?"

"Did you ask me a question?" Did this mean I had ticked the first sign: short-term memory issues?

"Yes. Didn't you hear it?"

"Hear what?" Confusion. That was another sign, wasn't it? Oh God, I was really losing my mind. I wasn't ready for this stage in life.

"Didn't you hear it?" she shouted.

I put my fingers into my ears. "I'm not deaf."

My ears were ringing. Was that a sign? I reached for the papers from the printer tray, but it was empty. What the fuck? I'd just printed them, hadn't I?

"I disagree." She glanced around the office. "Where's the robot lady?"

Robot lady? Now I was concerned that Sarah was also experiencing dementia. One of the symptoms was the inability to find the correct words when speaking. I was almost certain she had not intended to say robot lady. I brought the website back up. This time I was for sure going to print myself a copy of the list, but my phone buzzed with a reminder. I looked down at my desk, seeing the printed pages. I wasn't losing my mind completely. Or did moving them but not remembering tick another box?

"Seriously, where is she?" Sarah was searching for something in the office, moving books off the side tables.

This couldn't be a good sign. Were both of us heading for trouble?

Our kids weren't old enough to take care of us. Not that I wanted to burden our children, but it kinda served them right, considering how much trouble they caused us daily. What were the odds the four of them could properly care for two ailing parents while continuing to attend elementary school? Would they let us starve?

Sarah rooted under one of the couch cushions, pulling out the listening device I hated having under my roof. "Did you do this?"

I shook my head, though I wasn't entirely convinced I was being truthful. I hated the thing, but I'd been trying really hard these days to stay on Sarah's good side. Sarah had insisted on buying multiple devices so we could have one in every room. She used them like an intercom system to make announcements, and the kids loved to ask random questions and make the devices talk. Personally, I assumed they were a means of being spied on by our corporate overlords 24/7. There was definitely a possibility I'd put the device in the cushions in a fit of pique. But if questioned further, I was blaming my dementia.

"It was probably one of the kids," I said, hoping this totally plausible explanation would get her off my back. Then something started to click in my head. "Oh, I did hear your voice, but you sounded underwater or something. I thought I was losing my mind."

Glancing at the print-out of dementia symptoms, I laughed at my paranoia.

Sarah's eyes narrowed, and her lips pursed. "Jury's out on that one. I asked if you're ready."

"For what?"

Sarah closed her eyes, inhaled deeply, and then slowly released the air from her lungs. "We're taking the kiddos to see a Disney flick. Are you ready?"

"Do any animals die? Disney films trigger me. I mean, *Bambi*—what the fuck was that? Darker than dark."

From the way Sarah sucked in her lips, I suspected she was stifling a laugh. "Lucky for you, we're not seeing *Bambi*. We are going to see one of your favorites, though."

"My favorite is *Mickey's Christmas Carol*. Are we celebrating Christmas in July? Except, it's not July." It was only one day away, meaning my life was zooming toward a sad conclusion. Was Walt Disney nearing forty when he made Bambi?

"Sadly, it's not that one. Your other favorite."

A grin broke out across my face. *"The Little Mermaid?* The new one?"

She shook her head.

Disappointment flooded me, but I took one last stab, *"Beauty and the Beast?"*

"Frozen."

I groaned. "That's not my favorite at all. Not even in the top ten. It's like a million years old, which I know because I've seen it a million times. And don't bother telling me the others are older. I don't want to hear it."

"True, but it's the kids' turn to choose the movie, so buck up. This is about the kids. Not you."

"But—"

"Let it go, Lizzie." Sarah hummed a few bars of the dreaded song.

I laughed despite myself. "I hate you. I'm going to have that in my head for days now."

"Drop the act. I know deep down, you love the movie and the song. I've watched you bob your head every time, all one million of them."

"Because of the kids!" I got to my feet. "Are we at least going to the theater that serves a full menu of food?"

"We are."

"This day is looking up!" I put my hand up for a high five.

"After the movie, we're going to Tracy's for a barbecue. It's Owen's birthday party." Sarah slapped my palm.

"Are you saying I get movie popcorn, birthday cake and, the possibility of not doing dishes tonight?"

Sarah's eyes twinkled. "She used paper plates last time, so fingers crossed!"

"Should we feel guilty that we're contributing to the end of the world, or celebrate the fact we don't have chores? The older I get, the more torn I get about those choices."

"Tell you what. Blame me. You love to blame me for things. That way, you can stay in a good mood."

"You're such a good wife!" I kissed her cheek.

"I knew it!" Sarah was gloating, but why, I wasn't sure.

"What? I always tell you that."

"Not that. You were humming 'Let it go' just now. You, my darling curmudgeon, are a complete and total fraud." Sarah was grinning from ear to ear. "You love that movie, and you know it."

My brilliant response was, "Pffft!"

CHAPTER TEN

As we left the theater, it took a few seconds for my eyes to adjust to the bright daylight. We had arrived right before the show started, meaning we had a trek to the car. *Before Kids Lizzie* never showed up seconds before the lights went off. She would have been there in time to grab a parking spot in the front row and been most of the way through her popcorn and drink before the lights dimmed for the previews. But I had grown so accustomed to the new routine of dashing from the far end of the lot and squeezing into our seats halfway through the final trailer that I wasn't even very bothered by it anymore.

Was it time to admit *Before Kids Lizzie* was good and dead?

On our trek across the parking lot, all four kids broke out into a rousing rendition of "Let it Go," and gosh darn if it wasn't catchy. Soon, both Sarah and I joined in the fun. Sarah gave me a knowing look but didn't call me out in front of the children. Even so, I knew for certain *Before Kids Lizzie* was gone for good.

Having kids had changed me forever, hopefully for the better. At least 86.567 percent of the time.

"Now what?" Ollie asked, after buckling into the seat right behind me, the driver.

"We just saw a movie. Isn't that enough for the day?" I teased.

"No. I want funner."

"Funner than the movie?" I clicked my seatbelt, waiting for Sarah to close the last door after she ensured Calvin was actually buckled in. The kid even resisted common sense and the law. "We can chat about history. That would be fun."

"No one thinks that's fun," Ollie griped, kicking the back of my seat.

"Olivia Rose!" Sarah, who stood with the door open and had a front row seat to Ollie's antics, admonished our precocious child. "Do not kick!"

"I had hoped you'd come to my defense," I pouted as Sarah slammed her door after taking her seat. "Tell her history is fun."

"That's right. History is fun!" Sarah pressed her hands together, looking the opposite of enthused.

"Mockery. Just what the day was missing." I winked at Sarah.

"What are we doing again?" I peeked in the rearview mirror and saw Olivia wringing her hands, her eyes imploring me to give her an answer that didn't involve history. "At least the acting lessons are working."

Ollie made a seated bowing motion.

"We're going to Owen's house for a barbecue." Sarah looked into the back of the SUV. "So that means all of you will be on your best behavior."

"Yes!" Fred pumped a fist. Outside of the family, Owen was Freddie's best friend.

"I hate Owen. He's weird," Ollie whined.

I guessed from Sarah's quick reaction, Olivia went to kick the back of my chair again, but Sarah blocked her with a hand.

"Wow. You put yourself in danger to save me." I peeked at Sarah's hand to see if there was a mark. Ollie was quite the kicker.

"Correction, all of us but Olivia will be going to Owen's house," Sarah declared.

"That's not fair!" Ollie screeched.

"That's life, kiddo." Sarah turned around, her chest heaving up and down in anger. Truth be told, the sight of it did things to me that really weren't appropriate when I was supposed to be driving an SUV full of kids to a birthday party.

"Fine," Ollie grumped. "I don't like barbecues anyway."

Again, I checked the mirror to witness Ollie digging her butt firmly into her seat, placing both feet on the edge of the cushion so she could hug her knees.

"You hate hot dogs?" I asked, genuinely curious, but when Sarah shot me a *what the fuck are you doing* look, I realized I'd made a mistake. The hot dogs were not the most important topic at the moment.

"Only losers hate hot dogs," came Ollie's retort.

I had to hand it to the kid. When she made a stand, she went all in. And, I had to wonder who hated hot dogs in our family. Sarah hardly ate them, but did she hate them?

Sadly, Sarah wasn't the type of mom to get tangled with the least important aspect and stayed on the parenting task. "Drive to my mom's first. We'll drop off Ollie, and then the rest of us will have fun at Owen's."

"That seems mean—I mean to your mom. I agree Ollie shouldn't go." I, for one, loved grilled hot dogs, but I didn't want to ruin Sarah's mom's afternoon because my daughter was being a pill. "I'll stay home with Olivia. We'll work on a history project together. Maybe something about child labor in the Industrial Revolution Age."

Sarah burst into laughter. "I might put you in charge of punishing the children from now on."

By the time Sarah pulled out of our driveway, leaving Ollie and me standing outside the house, my daughter's mood had drastically changed from defiance to sullen resignation. Part of me felt bad for the kid. I, too, had experienced having my mouth run out ahead of my good sense, getting me into more trouble than I'd intended. Poor kid came by it naturally, for sure.

I motioned for her to sit on the retaining wall. "Do you regret saying what you did about Owen?"

"Ummm... he's different." Ollie's eyes were on the ground, her words mumbled.

"He's autistic. Like Fred and me."

"But I know you two," Ollie argued, a frown wrinkling her little face.

"You do. Since birth, in fact."

"I've known Fred longer." She cracked a sheepish smile.

"All the way back to the womb, which is why you protect him when other kids tease him. Here's the thing, though. Owen doesn't have a sibling to come to his rescue. And I know from his mom that not all the kids at school are kind to Owen. Do you think that's right?"

"I guess not." She kicked her feet in the air. A small act of rebellion about having to sit for this lecture.

"Look, kiddo. Being different can be hard, but it's also beautiful. You love acting and tennis. Some people might find that weird. You know why? Because it's easier to make fun of people than to get to know them. Have you tried getting to know Owen?"

Her nostrils flared. "All he talks about is dinosaurs."

"Dinosaurs are cool, dude. You like seeing them in museums."

"That's different." She looked away.

"How?" I sat on the wall next to her.

"It's… it's educational."

It was hard not to laugh at her weak attempt to explain why it was okay to like dinosaurs in some situations and not others.

"I think it's a shame we're missing his birthday."

"It's his birthday?"

I nodded, pretty certain I was on the money with that one. Hadn't Sarah mentioned it? Did I see it on the dreaded calendar?

Ollie's shoulders slumped. "I like birthday parties."

"They're pretty cool."

"Will everybody get gifts?"

"You're supposed to bring a gift for the birthday boy or girl—" I stopped for a beat, adding, "or person," not sure if Ollie and Fred had nonbinary schoolmates. It was taking some serious rewiring of my brain to make this change, but as someone who never felt like they fit in, I wanted to be as inclusive as possible of everyone.

"No, I mean the bag we get to take home at the end," Ollie explained as if I'd never been to a party. She wasn't far off the mark, but I'd helped make these bags for my kids' birthday parties, so I did know what they were.

"Party favors, you mean? Yes, the guests might get those. I don't know, really." I rubbed my chin, thinking. "What if, instead of missing the party completely, we go right now and get Owen a gift just from you on the way? Tomorrow, you can do some extra chores to pay for the gift, and then write a letter to me explaining why you should be kind to all people, not only your siblings. Do we have a deal?"

"Deal!" She hopped down. "Hurry. I don't want to miss the cake."

Funny. I'd been thinking the same thing. This kid truly took after me.

CHAPTER ELEVEN

"Where is that article I printed?" I asked myself, shuffling papers on my desk.

I was working on a lecture for the fall, and a week prior, I'd stumbled upon an article that was a godsend. So, naturally, I couldn't find it.

Growling, I grabbed at a pile of papers to my left, feeling something hard underneath.

What the...?

Pulling out the object from deep within the stack, my heart jolted like a rhino was charging for me.

Actually, I have no idea what would happen if a rhino charged after me. I can only assume I would freeze up in much the same way as I did when I pulled a vibrator from the depths of my research. I'd plugged it in to charge and covered it to keep it hidden, but I'd forgotten about it completely.

How did one forget about a hot pink sex toy on

their desk in the library when kids were in the house? Honestly, I must have been the worst parent on the planet, not to mention terrible wife. I was supposed to pack for my weekend away with Sarah before I went to bed that night, and I'd purchased this device to surprise her. If it hadn't been for dumb luck, I would have left it behind.

Then again, dumb luck was an important corollary to Lizzie's Law. If it weren't for bad luck and dumb luck, I'd have no luck at all.

But when it came to using a vibrator to rock Sarah's world, the whole purpose behind buying the thing in the first place, I couldn't afford to leave anything to chance. I'd need to try it out—not in *that* way, but I wanted to make sure I knew how to turn it on and what to expect on my own before getting anyone else involved.

Glancing at the closed door, I hesitated for a long second before pressing the button on the base.

"Jesus!" My fingers went numb almost instantly as the device hummed.

Did people really like this? It seemed that if it was too much for my hand, it would be overkill for... other bits.

I knew it was sometimes euphemistically called a personal massager, but I hadn't expected it to have the power of one of those vibrating chairs you could pay to sit in at the mall. How many times had I wished I'd had one of those when my neck started acting up recently?

All of a sudden, it was like a light switched on in my brain. I might not have a great desire to stick this little pink device between my legs, but I sure could think of a location it would do wonders.

Grasping it in one hand, I applied it to my neck, letting out a tiny moan. My shoulders were always stiffer than stiff, with one particular site that had the knot the size of Uranus. Not that I knew anything about the planet, but I liked to think of the knot as a pain in the ass.

Pressing it harder into the knot, I closed my eyes. I wasn't orgasming or anything, but the experience was almost as good. Sarah had been encouraging me to get a massage to help ease the pain, but I didn't like the idea of being naked on a table with a stranger.

Could this little thing be the solution?

Sadly, it wasn't why I'd gotten it. I was going to have to tell Sarah about it, of course. And once it had been used for—well, you know—I couldn't imagine wanting to put it on my neck again. That just felt wrong.

Unless…

My plan wasn't fully formed when the door handle started to move, bursting in on my thoughts and filling me with panic. I had been wrong before. This was definitely what being chased by a rhino would be like. My heart was going at least twice the speed it had been when I'd come across the vibrator unexpectedly. I frantically tried to switch the thing off, struggling because my fingers tingled so much I couldn't get them to obey a simple command.

The door started to swing open, but I hadn't managed to turn the thing off, so I did the only thing I could think to do to keep from getting caught. I put it between my thighs to hopefully muffle the sound. Instantly, tears sprang to my eyes as my entire lower body began to pulse.

"Are you packed yet?" Sarah swigged a water bottle. "It's bloody hot today."

"No and yes." I choked between each word, barely holding it together.

She started to speak but cocked her head to the side. "What's that sound?"

"What sound?"

I have to admit. It was hard to concentrate with the vibrator going full steam ahead between my legs. It wasn't near my clit, but I did start to get an inkling as to why people might like it. Perhaps I had been too hasty in dismissing its primary purpose.

"Is there a fly or something in here?" Sarah swatted the air. "Something is buzzing."

"It's summer. There are always flies. I'll be upstairs in a few minutes to pack." I squirmed in my chair, praying she would turn around and leave.

She did not.

"You honestly don't hear that buzzing?"

"Nope. Do you think you're getting tinnitus?"

She stuck a finger in one of her ears, giving it a shake. "I thought that was more of a ringing thing."

I shrugged. Meanwhile, I slipped a hand between my legs and did my best to locate and press the off button. Finally, mercifully, I was met with success.

"It's gone now." Sarah removed her finger from her ear. "I really hope that doesn't become a regular thing."

"When's your next physical?" I made a show of scratching at my knee so as to avoid suspicion for why I'd moved my hand so quickly from the desk to my lap.

"Not 'til October."

I didn't know what to say, mostly because I felt shitty about lying and making her think something was wrong with her when it clearly was not. How, though, was I supposed to surprise Sarah on our trip if I told her the truth?

"I'm going to bed. We're leaving early tomorrow, so don't stay up too late."

"Gotcha."

On her way to the door, Sarah turned around right when I tried to slip the device into the pocket of my shorts. "Do you hear it now?"

"Not at all." Given that the vibrator was off, I didn't have to lie this go around. "You really should mention this to your doctor. Do you need to make an earlier appointment?" Because now I really did think she had some hearing problems.

"I'm probably overtired and hearing things. Don't forget to pack for tomorrow. I want to get out of Dodge at daybreak."

The door closed, and I waited several minutes before switching the vibrator back on to work on the knot some more. For a little thing, it packed a punch just where I needed it to.

CHAPTER TWELVE

"Two nights away from the kids!" Sarah tossed herself down on the bed in the hotel overlooking the water in Rockport. She cupped her ear. "Do you hear that blessed sound?"

I strained, not noticing anything in particular.

"That is the sound of no kids fighting, and if you try really hard, you can hear the water even with the windows closed."

I opened the door to the deck that overlooked the ocean, the room filling with the sound of waves and ocean birds. "Better?"

"Much." Sarah placed her hands under her head, closing her eyes.

Outside on the deck, I checked out the view. The water lapped the rocky coastline, the level low. A black bird sat on one of the larger rocks. Taking my phone out, I tried to zoom in, but it was too far away to figure out what type of bird it was. All I knew was it wasn't a seagull. At least not like any I'd seen.

Stepping back into the room, I asked, "What do you want to do?"

Sarah's mouth was wide open, and it didn't take a rocket scientist to figure out she was dead to the world. As if determined to prove this theory correct, she let out a loud snore.

Okay, this was not how I'd pictured us starting our weekend away together. It was only half past three, and I wasn't the type who could take a nap, so I reached into my bag for a book.

Out on the deck, I leaned back in a white plastic chair, putting my feet up on the railing, and dove into my reading. There was a slight breeze with a chill to it, and the clouds rolling in were dark and heavy. Sure enough, it started to rain. I stayed put, though. The view was calming, and for the most part, I stayed dry aside from my feet and flip-flops. How often would I be able to read in peace and quiet on a deck overlooking the water?

I absolutely adored all of my kids and my wife, but I did miss Lizzie time. Feeling slightly guilty by that thought, I turned the page of my book, the world around me slipping away.

"Whatcha reading?" Sarah stood on the deck, stretching her arms overhead.

"Fuck, you startled me." I rested the book against my chest, uncertain how much time had passed. "To answer your question, *An American Beauty*. It's a gilded age novel about a woman who became the richest woman in the country."

"I hope you're taking notes."

"This is just for fun," I explained, "but Willow mentioned it on the podcast."

"I meant about becoming the richest woman."

"It's fun in fiction, not real life." I closed the book and set it beside me, knowing my reading time was done. "How'd you sleep?"

Sarah took the seat next to me. "Hard. Sorry about that."

"No need to apologize. We're here to relax."

"We're here for Sarah and Lizzie time," she corrected, "and I fell sound asleep. You must be so disappointed in me."

"Of course not," I assured her. Did that make me feel guilty for relishing my Lizzie time instead of being upset at her for napping? Yes, but only slightly. "What do you think of that place by the water for dinner?"

That seemed to be the safest way to direct the conversation instead of blurting, "I'd really like to finish this chapter, so zip it." I was thinking it, naturally, but at least I'd gotten a little bit better over the years at not saying things out loud that should be kept silent. Sometimes.

"Sounds nice, but I think you need reservations." Sarah yawned again. "We could try somewhere else."

"No need." I grinned. "I made a reservation

yesterday. I read someplace that it had the best view around."

"Food, sex, and scenic views." Sarah returned my grin.

I put a finger to my lips, shushing her loudly. "I don't think everyone needs to know that."

"First of all, who? We're totally alone on this deck." Sarah shook her head, laughing. "Second, it's why everyone is here."

"Do you think we'll hear them?" That thought made my skin crawl.

"I brought a sound machine, but I'm not sure we'll need ocean sounds with—" She finished her statement by pointing at the water. "I'm hoping they hear us, though."

My eyes widened. "Why in the world would you hope for that?"

"Because I'm planning to rock your world, and I seem to recall you promising to do the same."

She was right. I had made that promise. And I had a few things to make up for, not that she had any idea. For one thing, I'd marked my last sex reminder off the calendar without following through. And it was possible I'd left a certain something at home in my office that I'd intended to pack. I still planned to follow through on my word and rock her world. I'd just have to do it the old-fashioned way. Hopefully, my neck wouldn't give out.

"We should get dinner first. Hard to rock each

other when we're hungry." Almost as soon as I'd said it, an alarm sounded from inside the room. "That's my phone telling us it's time to leave for our reservation. I'd better go turn it off."

"I've got it," she said, darting back into the room as I slowly extricated myself from the plastic chair. A moment later, the phone went silent.

"Ready?" I asked, holding my hand out for my phone.

Sarah gave me a slightly puzzled look as she handed it over but didn't say anything as we headed out the door.

CHAPTER THIRTEEN

After a wonderful dinner, we returned to the hotel and sat on the deck outside of our room. Sarah slowly sipped at the red wine I poured her in a plastic cup I'd packed.

"This is one of my faves." She held the glass up so I could see the ghost in a bubble bath holding a glass of red wine exclaiming, "Boo-ble bath make me fine."

"Do you think the glass is a dead giveaway you need mommy juice even when away from the kids?" I teased.

"I think the bags under my eyes are enough to inform the world," she replied with a good-natured laugh.

I settled into the plastic chair next to her, squinting at her face, beautiful despite its traces of fatigue. "You don't have bags under your eyes."

"You're a damn liar. My bags have bags." Her smile

let me off the hook. "What other surprises do you have for me tonight? First, the hotel has this amazing deck. Second, you made reservations at the nicest restaurant in town. Third—" She flourished the wine glass. "This was a really nice touch."

"I figured since we don't have to jump out of bed at first light, you could indulge a bit." I stretched out my legs. "I could get used to hearing the waves. For real. Not a sound machine."

"And it's not as hot here." Sara stretched her arms above her, letting out a small sigh. "Maybe we should move to the coast."

"Not sure I want to be along the water, what with climate change and all that. We might have beachfront property soon enough where we are." I laughed at my own joke.

"It worries me." Sarah took another sip, her tone somber. "What will it be like for our grandchildren?"

"Hey now. Aren't you the one who's always telling me things aren't so bad? We don't have to move to Mars?" Again, I laughed, but it was more forced this time. Sarah was supposed to be the optimist. She balanced me out. I couldn't afford for her to go to the dark side on me.

"You haven't answered my question yet. What other surprises do you have for me?" She eyed me like she was expecting something big. My stomach clenched a little as I sensed I was on shaky ground, uncertain what she expected of me.

"Aside from being the rational one for a change? None," I confessed. "I'm afraid the wine was my only weak attempt for romance."

Sarah rolled the glass in her hands. "I know you're lying."

I swiveled my head to face her, concern creasing my brow. "Pretty sure I'm not. Do I need to run out to get —something. Ice cream? Pastries?"

Disappointment fell over Sarah's features. "Don't tell me you forgot to pack the vibrator?"

My jaw dropped. "I don't have a vibrator," I protested with horror, not pretending in the least.

She grinned victoriously. "Don't be shy. In case you've forgotten, we're married." She held up her left hand to show me her ring.

"I haven't." I displayed my own wedding band. "But there isn't a vibrator in my bag. Why do you think there is one?"

Sadly, this was the truth, and I was very quickly realizing the magnitude of my mistake.

"Lizzie, I saw the order on Amazon when I was checking a delivery. You don't have to be embarrassed."

"You just assumed it was me who ordered it?"

Sarah's eyes widened. "I sure hope it wasn't one of the kids, or we'll have to have a talk. But to be fully honest, I also heard you testing it out last night in the library. Were you sitting on it or something? It took restraint not to bust you right then and there."

"Hold up a sex—er sec. Did you lie about hearing things on the way out the door?" I fully embraced my indignation.

"It's possible I was messing with you. Also, you just confirmed you have the vibrator. So, should we move this inside?" She used her bedroom voice all the while batting her long lashes.

"I didn't confirm anything. And it's not here," I mumbled, knowing somehow I was on the edge of a very deep abyss. "It's still in my desk drawer."

Sarah's face fell even more than before as the truth sank in. "You forgot to pack it."

"No—I mean yes. Exactly."

Disappointment morphed into something altogether different as Sarah leveled her dark brown eyes on mine. Even in the fading light, I knew she was well past suspicious and on the verge of murderous. Why had I planned a weekend away next to the ocean? It wouldn't take much for her to roll my body down the rocks and let the tide do the rest.

"When you give me two answers, I know the second is a lie. Which only leads me to believe you didn't pack it on purpose." Her lips settled into a grim line, and my life flashed before my eyes. She was onto me, and I was not going to survive this encounter.

"Why would I do that?" I protested despite knowing I was doomed. I mean, I knew the reason I'd actually done it, but it'd help to know if she did. Was this the time to bring up all the early onset dementia boxes I ticked? Maybe I could win some pity.

She folded her arms, the daggers shooting from her eyes were almost lethal. There would be no pity from her.

"Okay. Alright. I kinda didn't forget—"

"Bullshit," she spat out. "There's no *kinda* about it."

I hated that she knew I was lying, but I didn't want to confess the truth. Not when she was staring at me like she wanted to tear all of my hair out, one strand at a time.

"Explain, Lizzie."

"I have no idea how—"

Sarah shifted menacingly in her chair.

"I didn't want to share, okay? I tried it out last night. Not how you think, though!" I rushed to add. I scooted my chair a little bit to the left, which was sadly closer to the water's edge. I eyed the large rocks, wondering how much it would hurt when my head crashed into one after a sexually frustrated Sarah pushed me over the railing.

Luckily for me, she motioned for more information instead of letting me plunge to my fate.

"I tried it out on my neck. It worked on that knot. The one you keep saying I need a professional for." Would that make Sarah less murderous?

"Oh, you need a professional," she spat.

Guess not, but I continued to dig in. "I don't think

I do now. That's the beauty of what I'm trying to tell you. That hot pink thing works miracles."

Sarah's eyes turned to slits. "Not the kind of professional help I meant."

"Therapy?" I took a stab at what she meant.

"We're past that point. You're going to need a whole team of professionals to put you back together." Somehow, she kicked her menacing glare to a whole new terrifying level. "I don't understand why the knot in your neck equates to not packing the vibrator you bought for our sexy weekend away."

"I don't want it to get... ya know... gross." As soon as the words were out, I knew I'd made a tremendous error.

"I'm sorry?" She jerked back like she'd been struck. "Are you implying I'm gross? That sex with me is gross?"

"What? No. Not one bit." How did she get there? This had gone even worse than I'd expected, and way faster, too. I couldn't keep up.

"They're meant to be cleaned. You know that, right? It's not a one and done, disposable kind of thing." I'm not sure I'd ever seen Sarah's face contort like that before.

"I can fix this. I'll order you one of your own." I pulled out my phone. "What color would you like so we don't get them mixed up? They have green and blue—"

"You're unbelievable, you know that?" Sarah's

voice cracked, and an odd sparkle suggested there were tears gathering in her eyes. "I mean, I didn't believe it at first when I saw that you have a reminder on your phone for sex—"

"Have you been snooping?" I demanded, momentarily forgetting I was the one in trouble here.

"I saw it when the restaurant reminder went off!" She was yelling now, and I glanced along the deck to determine if any of the lights in the other rooms turned on. They had not, which meant my murder would go unwitnessed and unsolved. Sarah had probably been planning it long enough to know how not to get caught. "A reminder for sex. Do you know how that makes me feel? Like a chore. What's your nightly checklist? Take out the trash. Brush teeth. Fuck Sarah. I'm not something that needs to be checked off a list."

"It says *hubba bubba,*" I offered in a strangled whisper. It had seemed like such a brilliant solution that I'd never stopped to think how Sarah might interpret it otherwise. But what did it matter if I needed a reminder so long as the goal was achieved?

Sarah stared at me. Hard. For many seconds. Her chest was heaving up and down. Very inconveniently, I no longer needed the reminder on my phone. I was turned on good by what I saw. Sadly, I was pretty sure my sex life was dead for my remaining years.

The very definition of Lizzie's Law.

Finally, Sarah stood. "I don't like our sleeping

arrangements. I'm going to speak to the front desk person. Pack your stuff."

Before I could ask what was wrong with the room, Sarah slammed the door.

I was 99.987 percent certain it wasn't the room but me. And I could sort of see her point when I looked at it a certain way. That wasn't to say she was right, but maybe I had been more going through the motions than actually trying to reestablish a real connection between us. Maybe I'd been more concerned about checking off boxes than letting myself feel the complicated rush of emotions and sensations that could overwhelm me in my most vulnerable states.

She returned five minutes later, grinning. But not a comforting kind of grin. "There's a room with two double beds available. Grab your bag."

"We're moving rooms. Why?"

"Oh no. You are moving. I plan on taking up every inch of this nice big bed, sleeping with the window open, so I can hear the waves while I rock my own world. No vibrator required." She tossed a key attached to a big plastic thing with the number seven embossed in gold.

I started to protest, but she made a zip-it motion across her lips. I'd seen her do it with the kids, and I had to admit it was effective.

Without further protest, I shoved my things into my backpack. When I turned around, Sarah stood on the deck, her hands on the railing. I counted to twenty, hoping she'd turn around and stop me from leaving. She didn't.

It occurred to me as I trudged to my new room that I had time to finish that chapter now. I worried that wasn't the only thing I was about to finish.

CHAPTER FOURTEEN

I spent much of the day wandering Rockport on my own, brooding about where I'd gone wrong. Like so many times before, in hindsight, I could see it all so clearly. Sadly, I was pretty sure that given it all to do over again, I would fuck up in exactly the same way. Or maybe in new and different ways. Who knew? It seemed to be my talent. Sarah finally had to be around me when we drove home Sunday evening. In complete and total silence. She didn't even allow the radio to be on. At least, I didn't dare ask if I could turn it on.

It seemed every family in Massachusetts was heading home from a weekend away at exactly the same time. The traffic crawled to the point I felt like we were going backward.

Just what this miserable weekend away needed. The two of us being trapped in a car.

Sarah stared straight ahead, her breathing steady.

Too steady. Like contemplating murder steady. Just because she'd never murdered me before with all the times I'd thought she might didn't mean she wouldn't one day. Today might be that day.

When we got home, would Sarah have me sleep in the apartment instead of in our bed? I still hadn't found time to put a puzzle together. With Ethan and his family arriving in seven days, I'd better get a jump on it or miss out this year. Somehow, this opportunity didn't cheer me like it should have. So far, the Summer of Lizzie was speeding at warp speed to Single-Mom Lizzie.

Would Sarah start divorce proceedings over a vibrator? What would she tell everyone? What would I? How could I find a lawyer and explain exactly where I went wrong? They'd probably heard more than their fair share of wacky marriage drama, but this? Surely this case would be unique.

A driver in a BMW cut me off, and I laid on my horn.

"Trying to get us shot?" Sarah glared at me.

Not making eye contact, I took my hand off the middle of the steering wheel. "He cut me off. He has no right to shoot me. I have every right—" I stopped myself from saying more. I was not scoring any points right now.

"People are disappointing."

I swallowed. Sarah wasn't the one who said things like this. I was. Would it be hard to find an apartment that had enough room for the kids to visit? Would I permanently move into the apartment over the garage?

All because of a vibrator? This was the epitome of Lizzie Luck.

After three hours and thirteen minutes, we arrived at our home.

Without a word, Sarah got out of the vehicle and went inside. Was she already mentally dividing up our belongings?

When I entered the house, the kids rushed toward me, their little arms in the air. I knelt down for a massive hug.

"Are you crying?" Freddie asked.

"Allergies," I fibbed.

Sarah wasn't in the entryway, and I heard her voice drifting in from the kitchen. I assumed her mom was in there, and that they were probably discussing the finer points of restraining orders and legal custody. Or how to roll up my body in a rug and bury it in the woods. I could see Rose being willing to get in on that plan, especially if she found out about the vibrator debacle.

Rose rounded the corner. She was not holding a shovel, so I was probably safe for now. "Did you have a good weekend, Lizzie?"

"What did Sarah say?" I asked, my eyes darting around the room in avoidance.

"She said she had the best lobster roll." Rose canted her head to the side.

"Yeah, same here."

"You hate lobster." Rose's tone told me she wasn't easily fooled.

Honestly, of all the things, she had to remember *that* detail about me? Maybe because I wasn't all that suave when it came to things that grossed me out. Clearly.

"I meant that the weekend was good. Not the lobster roll." I added, "Thanks for watching the kiddos."

"Anytime." Rose kissed each one on the top of the head. "I'll see you all tomorrow."

"For ice cream?" Demi asked.

"I think you have an addiction, my Demitasse." I ruffled her hair. "Let's get all of you to bed. What story are we reading?"

"Mommy usually reads to us." Freddie sounded suspicious.

"Mommy is tired." *Of me*, I thought but managed not to say. "I'll read tonight."

There was a noise in the kitchen, which sounded like the glug of wine being poured into a glass.

"Did you see any whales?" Fred asked as he ascended the stairs.

"No, but we didn't go whale watching." We'd planned on it, but Sarah texted she had a headache, and I wasn't too keen on getting seasick on my own. "Would you like to go whale watching?"

He bobbed his head.

"Let's add it to our summer fun list." Right next to getting a lawyer, apparently. That would be a barrel of laughs, for sure.

"And sharks!" Calvin bounced on the balls of his feet. "I want to wrestle a shark."

Of course, he did.

After closing the book, when Calvin finally quit fighting sleep, I scooped up my youngest from Fred's bed and carried Calvin to his own in the next room. Next, I got Demi from Ollie's bed.

There wasn't a light on in our bedroom.

Should I go to bed or find Sarah to talk about the vibrator? Better yet, what if I suggested we use the vibrator together? Would that save my marriage?

Before I could decide, there was a knock on the front door.

It was nearly nine. Who could be knocking now? Process servers didn't work this late, did they? Not to mention so quickly? We'd only been home an hour at the most. Plus, it was a Sunday. Maybe Sarah had called a hit man. I doubted they had strict rules about working on the Lord's day.

The knocking sounded again, and I froze at the top of the stairs, not wanting to find out.

There were footsteps. The squeaking hinge of the front door, and then a squeal. A happy one. Kind of an over-the-top response for a hit man, even if she was excited to finally off me.

"Ethan!"

That got my feet moving, and I practically ran down the stairs.

"You're early!" I didn't wait for an answer, throwing my arms around his neck. For many years, Ethan was my sounding board, and I needed his opinion about the vibrator situation pronto. It wasn't until I hugged Casey that I realized moving into the apartment was off the table for not one week, but two.

There were always the couches in the library, but that spelled trouble for my neck.

"What happened?" Sarah asked, hugging Lisa. "I thought you had an epic sightseeing itinerary planned."

"Have you ever driven across Nebraska?" Casey, who was nearly as tall as Sarah now, asked.

"Can't say that I have." Sarah answered honestly.

"Turns out there's not much to see," Casey replied. "Who'd have thought, right? Add in the air conditioning going kaput, and we put the pedal to the metal."

"And, we couldn't wait to see all of you." Lisa gave her daughter a look that I couldn't interpret.

"I'm hungry." Casey rubbed her stomach.

"I'm sure we can rustle something up."

"What about if we order a pizza? Will that take too long?" I directed the question to Casey. "The local place is good and delivers until midnight."

"I always have time for pizza." She wore a huge smile.

"We don't want to put you out." Delores, whom I didn't interact with much, shifted on her feet, standing to the side.

"We arrived a week early," Casey stated matter-of-factly. "We already have."

"Don't be silly. Pizza is the least we can do after your harrowing trek across the country." Sarah put an arm around Casey, leading her into the front room. "I want to hear all about it. You must have seen a few interesting things, right?"

"Well, we did see a Pony Express station. That was pretty cool. Did my postcard arrive? They stamp it there. I placed it into a leather bag." Casey bubbled with enthusiasm, not looking worse for the wear. "Where are the kids?"

"Sadly, they just went to bed, but they'll be stoked to see you in the morning." I pulled up the menu to our local pizza place. "Now what kind of pizza would you like."

"I don't care as long as there are olives."

I nearly gagged, but Sarah swooped in with a response.

"Olives? Perfect." Sarah flashed an evil smile, knowing I hated olives with a passion.

Lizzie's Law struck again.

CHAPTER FIFTEEN

"Ice cold Cracker Jacks, here." A man in a yellow shirt held up a brightly colored example. He had more stored in a bag slung across his chest as he walked up the stairs in the stands at Fenway Park.

"It's frozen?" I squinted at the red, blue, and white plastic bag. "Is that a new way to eat them? Like ice cream?"

Ethan laughed. "Glad to know you haven't changed."

I took my eyes off the baseball field down below and focused on Ethan. "What do you mean?"

"Nothing." He bit down on his lip. "I think the man was making a joke. I imagine when it's plus ninety degrees, and with this humidity, selling Cracker Jacks is a tough gig."

I wiped my brow on my sleeve. "Too bad. I was curious what Cracker Jack ice cream tasted like."

"Did someone say ice cream?" Demi shot out of her seat. Fortunately, she wasn't tall enough to block the view.

"After the game." I waved for Demi to sit back down, which she did with a hangdog expression that I chalked up to exhaustion.

It was day five since Ethan and his crew arrived, and Sarah had kicked it into high gear to show them everything about Massachusetts, including a game at Fenway. Somehow, my dad got us all a block of seats.

"I could go for some ice cream." Helen gave Demi a conspiratorial wink.

"Me too." My father got to his feet. "How many? Twelve?"

"I don't need one." Delores, who went by Lola—a fact I had been reminded of a couple of times already—adjusted her new green baseball hat.

"Me neither." Lisa swigged water from a bottle.

"Ten? Speak now or—" My dad laughed.

"I'll go with you." I got to my feet.

So did Ethan and Sarah.

We edged out of the aisle as quickly as possible so we didn't disrupt the people there to actually watch all the action, we headed down toward the area with all the concession stands.

"Charles and I will get in one line to avoid upsetting people by ordering ten ice creams. Lizzie and Ethan, get five chocolates with sprinkles." Sarah waved for my dad to join her.

Ethan and I joined a line, about fifteen deep.

"She hasn't thawed any," I commented, the smell of hot dogs, sausages, burgers, and fried dough overwhelming my senses.

"You might be the first person to get divorced because of a vibrator," Ethan said, much louder than he should have.

An older woman glanced over her shoulder. "I doubt that."

Ethan laughed.

I wanted to die.

Fortunately, that was all the woman had to say about the subject, so I was spared additional humiliation. Although, maybe I deserved it. I hadn't been able to decide. Was I at fault here, or the victim of an unreasonable amount of anger for something relatively minor? I could see it both ways.

"Have you tried talking to her?" Ethan took a step around a puddle of what I hoped was spilled beer.

There was a crack of a bat, and the crowd roared, before it turned to boos.

"Foul ball or pop-out," Ethan explained. "So, have you?"

"We haven't had a chance to talk. She's either dragging us to a museum or a national park, or she's answering text messages. She hasn't had a minute. Besides, what would I say?"

"I'd start with you're sorry."

"She shouldn't have looked at my order. Or my

phone." It was a flimsy excuse at best, and I knew it. I glanced across the way, where Sarah stood with a phone to her ear, plugging her free ear with a finger. "How big is this party supposed to be, anyway?"

"Party? What party?" Ethan tried escaping but nearly stepped in the dubious pool of liquid on the cement.

"You're a terrible liar. I told Sarah I didn't want a birthday party. More than once."

"She loves you. She's still trying to hold it together even if she hates your guts right now."

"That makes no sense. Did she tell you that?"

"No, and I'm exaggerating, but do yourself a favor. Talk to her tonight."

"I—I'm not ready." The truth was I was scared to an almost irrational degree, and I wasn't even certain why. Deep down, I knew I was catastrophizing the situation and that talking it through was the most sensible solution. That didn't make it any easier.

"Do you want to end up like that person?" Ethan jerked his head to a dad, who was wrangling three kids, two of them crying as the third kicked him in the shins. "He's putting up with the behavior. Ten bucks he's a divorced dad."

"Sarah's not going to divorce me. I—" My mind went blank about how I contributed to the household, not to mention my good qualities. Perhaps I hadn't been catastrophizing things after all.

Ethan wore a knowing smile, his tiny mustache mocking me.

That night, I placed my newly washed plastic Red Sox cap, the one that had held my ice cream with sprinkles—or jimmies as they liked to call them in Massachusetts—on my desk. The kids were in bed, and Ethan and his family had retired to the apartment over the garage.

I sat in my chair, trying to summon up the nerve to speak to Sarah.

My phone buzzed with a text.

Gabe might not make it.

It was from Sarah. Was she texting me from inside the house, or had she stepped out and I didn't hear? I wasn't sure, but I didn't think texting instead of walking down the hall and poking your head through the door to say something in person was a good sign. I tapped the top of the ice cream cup. Aside from Sarah staring daggers at me, it'd been a good day. Calvin was now convinced he could skip school and become a professional baseball player. I had to give it to the kid. He swung for the fences.

Maybe I should take a page out of his playbook.

I headed for our bedroom, finding Sarah sitting up in bed, texting furiously.

"What's wrong with Gabe?"

"His flight keeps getting canceled." She didn't look up from the phone. "Same with Janice and Bailey."

"Yeah, I've heard flying right now is a nightmare.

Ethan and his family did it the right way. At least they arrived."

Sarah nodded. This was not going well, and she was clearly not going to give me so much as an inch.

I worked my way across the room, each step falling heavily like my legs were turning to stone.

"We're leaving for the lake house tomorrow afternoon. I'll have to arrange for rides for everyone now." Sarah didn't look up.

"We can cover their ride shares." I sat on her side of the bed, putting my hand on her phone.

Sarah jerked it free.

"Please. We need to talk."

"About?" She at least set the phone to the side on my pillow.

"Rockport."

"It's a lovely seaside town." She moved to get her phone, still very much in a huff.

"I'm sorry. I am. It was selfish of me." I paused a second, uncertain whether to continue. But the smartest thing at this point seemed to be to get everything out at once. "You know, you've been mad at me all this time, without taking into account you haven't exactly been a saint yourself."

Sarah straightened up, a look of indignation on her face. "How are you going to pin this on me? You're the one who bought the damn thing and then decided I wasn't worthy of it."

"Not the vibrator." I took a deep breath. "I told you

116

several times, very clearly, that I didn't want a big fuss. For the entire day, you've been triaging these travel hiccups."

Sarah put a hand to her chest. "I'm gathering our loved ones at a lake house. How is that a crime?"

"On July fourteenth," I pressed. "Which happens to be my birthday."

"It's when everyone's free." Sarah's eyes dropped to the comforter, an undeniable sign of guilt.

I massaged my forehead. "Why is it okay for you to lie when it's not okay for me?"

"That's how surprise parties work. There has to be subterfuge!"

"I didn't want a fucking party." I shot to my feet, pacing our bedroom. "I hate surprises!"

"Tell you what, Lizzie. You don't have to go. You've battled me for I don't know how long not to be a part of this family. Stay home. We'll go without you." The words weren't shouted but said with such finality that they pierced my soul.

"A vibrator. That's what's causing this. A fucking vibrator!" I tossed my hands to the ceiling as if wanting divine intervention. "Why can't you admit you're wrong? Not about the vibrator but for ignoring my wishes. I don't like a fuss over my birthday. They bring so many bad memories. Like not getting a cake or any gifts when I was a kid."

"That's why I'm planning this." Sarah's voice cracked with emotion. "Because it breaks my heart that was your childhood. I want to throw you a party every day of your life so you know how amazing you are!"

"Then why do you want a divorce?"

"Who said I did?" Sarah tapped her thumb to each finger on her right hand, as if trying to add how I'd reached that conclusion.

"You've barely said a word to me since Ethan got here."

"Because I'm hurt." Her eyes glistened. "You hurt me."

"I—" I stood in the middle of our bedroom, unable to speak.

"If you want, I'll cancel the party. It's not like everyone can make it anyway." Her phone buzzed. "Gabe's on the plane!"

"How did you convince Gabe to leave the stores?"

"I said I was throwing you a birthday party."

I blinked, trying to process this. "There wasn't any bribery?"

Sarah tilted her head. "Why would I have to bribe your brother?"

"Because—I don't know anymore." I went and sat down next to her. "I didn't mean—I'm sorry I hurt you. I never want to do that." I threaded my fingers through hers.

"I'm sorry I planned this party. We can cancel."

"No. I think the kids are looking forward to the lake house." I rubbed my neck. "It sounds nice."

"Okay, we'll go, but we don't have to celebrate anything." Sarah checked her phone, doing a fist pump. "Janice and Bailey have a flight!"

"I can't remember the last time I saw Janice." I ran back through Sarah's offer not to have a celebration, a frown settling on my lips. "The kids will want birthday cake."

"Just the kids?" There was a ghost of a smile on her lips.

"I may not be a good person, but I'm not a monster. Who doesn't like cake?" I tightened my grip on Sarah's fingers. "You promise my gift isn't divorce papers?"

A soft chuckle shook Sarah's shoulders. "I really wish you wouldn't go immediately to the nuclear option every time we fight."

"You've met me, right? Hi, I'm Lizzie Petrie, and I overreact to everything." I stuck out my hand for her to shake.

She accepted it. "Sarah. I plan unwanted parties."

"Maybe you should seek help for that."

"There's clearly something wrong with me," she agreed. "Because no matter what you do, I can't stop loving you."

"You promise?"

"I do." She leaned up to kiss me, my heart fluttering with hope and relief.

Was my Lizzie luck turning around?

CHAPTER SIXTEEN

I stood on the shore of the lake, the cold water lapping the sand beneath my feet. The sky was beyond blue, with a scattering of tiny, puffy white clouds of the type kids put in drawings. A gentle breeze blew, chasing away the heat. A perfect day.

"Mommy! Look at me!" Demi jumped off a dock, splashing into the water and swimming toward Sarah.

"Great job, my Little Demitasse!" I gave her the thumbs-up.

Calvin cannonballed into the water, utterly lacking in fear.

Gabe and Allen, holding hands despite being full-grown men, launched themselves into the water, laughing.

"You're not getting in?" Janice joined me on the beach, a Diet Coke can in her hand.

"I'm enjoying watching, really. Everyone seems so

happy. Like they all fit together. I mean, look at Ethan with Casey on his shoulder and Lola with Lisa on hers. They're having a blast."

"Even Bailey." Janice's younger cousin swam up to Allen, dunking him below the water. "They're talking again. Did you know that?"

"I didn't. Allen's been living in Boston. I don't see him much." I raised my water bottle to take a sip. "I thought the long-distance thing became too much. Allen's looking at Harvard for grad school."

"So's Bailey." Janice put a hand on my shoulder. "Do you remember that feeling? Thinking of where to go for grad school? It seems like a lifetime ago, but not really because it also seems like just yesterday."

I nodded, a sense of wistfulness filling my chest. "I know what you mean. Half the time I feel ancient, the other half, I still feel like I'm twenty, ready to conquer the world—by that I mean, academia."

Janice laughed.

My dad and Freddie, along with Helen and Ollie, paddled by in kayaks, and I waved.

"It's good to see you, Lizzie," Janice said. "It's been too long."

I offered Janice a level gaze. "It really has. Now that we're on opposite coasts, it's—no, that's an excuse. We should make this a tradition. Every year, we all get together for a vacation."

"I'm down with that." Janice set her can down on the sand. "I'm going in."

I nodded, taking a seat in my red camp chair.

Sarah and Demi splashed their way out of the water, both of them squealing.

"Let me get you a towel." I got out of my chair, getting two towels from a table that was off to the side in the shade. I handed one to Sarah and wrapped the other around Demi before retaking my seat.

Demi climbed into my lap. Despite her being all wet, I wrapped my arms around her. "Chilly?"

She nodded, falling into my embrace.

Sarah pulled a chair next to mine. "What a beautiful spot."

"It is. Any chance you can book it for next year? Janice and I were chatting, and we've come to the agreement that all of us should get together once a year."

"Is that right?" Sarah wore a victorious smile. "Maybe we should head in her direction next time."

"Good idea."

"Demi! Come back!" Calvin bobbed in the water.

She shot off my lap, dumping the towel in the water.

Sarah shook her head as she grabbed the towel and wrung it out the best she could. "Where's my mom and Troy?"

"Playing checkers on the deck of their cabin." I let out a long, cleansing breath. "It's a shame every day isn't like this. I could get used to this feeling. Could you ask for a better sky and view?"

"It's paradise." Sarah waved to Calvin and Demi, both jumping off the dock again into the water.

"Not quite, but one thing would bring it a step closer." I held her gaze.

"I think I know where you're going, and don't fret, it's almost time for cake."

I raised my eyebrows. "You mean birthday cake?"

"Your birthday was yesterday. Today it's just cake."

"I can't believe Janice and Bailey sat on the tarmac for six hours before the plane turned back to the terminals. If we do head west next summer, we're driving. I want to see that Pony Express Station in Nebraska."

Sarah playfully groaned. I knew from experience she wasn't nearly as turned off by the idea as she pretended to be. In fact, chances were she'd be the first one to put her postcards in the leather bag and make a big show of it.

"It'll be good for the kids," I argued, because that was my role in this interaction. It was good to be back on solid ground, knowing where we each stood and how to navigate a conversation.

"What will?" Willow, with Maddie, joined us, bringing their own chairs.

"A road trip to the Pacific." Sarah scooted her chair closer to mine.

"Four kids and three thousand miles? I'll pass," Maddie said.

"Not me!" Willow bounced in her seat.

"Good luck getting out of it now." I stuck my tongue out at Maddie.

"You'll pay for this." Maddie shook a fist.

Gabe waved his hands over his head. "You made it!" He swam toward the shore.

The four of us swiveled our heads, my heart pounding in my throat. Was Peter standing behind me?

But there stood a tiny brunette.

Gabe tossed his arms around her before he dried off.

The woman leaned into the embrace.

"No complaint at all. That's new love," Maddie eyed the couple, and I had to wonder her internal thoughts since she'd dated Gabe briefly. So far, she had been with two of my brothers, which was a fact that still did my head in when I put too much thought into it.

Gabe, with an arm around the woman, said, "This is Avalon."

"I'm so glad you're here." Sarah got to her feet, hugging the woman.

I gave Maddie a puzzled look. Had they met before? I had no idea who this was. Gabe and I didn't talk much, but had Helen mentioned he was dating someone and I completely spaced it? Also, Avalon. I would have thought I'd remember that name. Ten bucks she was born and raised in Boulder.

"I wouldn't have if you hadn't texted me every five

minutes when I wanted to curl up in a ball and cry. Flying these days is practically a combat sport, and not being able to travel with Gabe was stressful." Avalon laughed.

"I was doing my best to keep track of everyone's flights and to help in any way I could. Gabe was losing his mind not being able to help, so I stepped in. I feel like we go back years now." Sarah gave Avalon another hug.

"Thanks for including me." Avalon leaned into the hug, clearly spent by her ordeal.

"We're all family here, right Lizzie?" Gabe grinned at me.

"Absolutely. The more the merrier." It must have been the whole lake experience because I wasn't lying. "How do you feel about a road trip next summer?"

CHAPTER SEVENTEEN

The sky turned a stunning orange and red as the sun dipped closer and closer to the horizon. I let out a contented sigh, rubbing my belly, filled with hot dogs, chips, and watermelon.

Life didn't get much better than this.

"Happy birthday to you."

I whipped around.

Sarah held a cake in her arms, so many candles valiantly flickering, fighting off the slight breeze.

Everyone continued singing, while Sarah set the sheet cake on the picnic table.

"I thought this was just cake, not birthday cake," I teased Sarah.

"Go on. Blow out the candles." Sarah leaned closer. "Don't forget to make a wish."

"It's already come true," I told her, and it was absolutely the truth.

"Smooth talker," she teased.

"Blow out the candles." Ollie already held a paper plate, presumably for the largest slice.

"Just for that," I told her, "I'm going to wait a little longer."

"Not too long. You're almost dead," Ollie quipped.

Everyone laughed, even me. I blew out the candles in one big breath, quite a feat considering how many there were. Was this what forty candles looked like? I would have gone for the ones shaped like numbers instead. This was likely to start a wildfire.

"Speech," Allen shouted through cupped hands, Bailey whacking him in the side.

"Nothing about the Nazis. There are children present." Ethan put his hands over his daughter's ears.

"Ignoring the resurgence of white nationalism in this country isn't the answer," Casey said, deadly serious.

"You've turned her into one of you," Ethan lobbed the statement at me.

"What does that mean?" I placed a hand on my chest, feigning innocence while bursting with pride.

"A pessimist," Ethan accused.

"I prefer realist. Now, where's my cake?" Casey stuck her plate out in a move that could have been stolen directly from my playbook.

"She does take after you," Sarah commented as she sliced off a piece, giving it to Casey. Ollie's annoyance at not being first was palpable, at least until she got the next one.

"Not letting you off the hook, Sister. Speech." Allen grinned.

I glanced around, and everyone looked expectantly at me.

Sarah at least seemed a bit mortified. Not enough to tell everyone to back off, but she was busy getting cake to the masses, so I guessed she couldn't do both at once. I would have to succumb and give the crowd what they wanted.

"Okay, I guess I can say a few words." I licked my lips, not sure what I was going to say. "Honestly, when I suspected Sarah was planning this bash, I wasn't happy. I didn't want a big party. I'm not big into birthdays, and turning forty—that's a big deal."

There was some rumbling.

I locked eyes with Rose. "Not that getting old is a problem."

"Careful," Rose cracked.

"Uh, Lizzie?" my dad spoke up, confusion on his face. "You're not forty."

I put up a hand. "No, it's okay. I can face it now. With all of you here to support me, what better way to enter middle age. I don't have to pretend to be younger than I am."

"That's lovely, sweetie." Sarah used the tone she employed when speaking to Calvin about not being in the same grade as Fred. "But, your dad's right. You're not forty."

I blinked.

"I'm older?" I could barely get the words out. How off was I? Forty-one? Forty-two? Oh, God…

"No, honey." Sarah put a hand on my arm. "You're younger."

"By how much?" My mind was racing. I'd been so certain I had this right. What year was it, anyway?

"Let me help you out," Maddie sassed. "You're thirty-eight."

"I'm thirty-eight? No. That can't be." I started counting on my fingers, giving up quickly. "Do all of you agree I'm not forty?" There were murmurs and nods all around.

"Did someone bring her birth certificate?" Maddie asked. "What am I saying? You don't math well, but given you're a historian, it seems like you should know dates."

"Old ones, yes."

"I'm going to have to caution you again, Lizzie." There was humor in Rose's tone. "Now, can the adults have cake?"

"If you're not forty yet, does that mean you can still naked cuddle?" Cal slanted his head, waiting for a response.

"Uh…?" My mind went blank. I was still processing the age news, and adding this on top of it was overloading the circuits.

Before I could jumpstart my brain, Cal turned to Freddie. "Mommy explained all about naked cuddling to me."

"What?" I shrieked. "Now, that's not—"

"It's when you hold Baby Yoda really close. But I'm thinking you can't do that when you get too old."

"Think again." Rose gave Troy's hand a squeeze.

My father exchanged a look with Helen that no child, no matter how old, should ever witness.

I wanted to swim to the other side of the lake. And stay there. Forever.

"I feel like your parenting lessons are different than ours." Ethan grinned.

"Do you need me to explain the birds and the bees to them?" Casey meant each word.

"Not yet, but we'll keep that in mind." What did Casey know about the birds and bees? I wanted to question Ethan, but would that open the floodgates to even more things I wish I never knew?

"Are you done with your speech?" Sarah asked, the knife hovering over the chocolate frosting.

I nodded, dumbstruck, my mind going back to the number of candles that had been on the cake.

All of this fretting I'd been doing, and I wasn't forty. That meant I was going to have to do it all over again in two years' time. Unless I used this as a lesson and decided to accept myself for whatever age I was and not worry about it again.

Come on. Who was I kidding?

Willow took over slicing duties, and Sarah pulled me to the side.

"You okay?"

"I'm not forty." Truly, I was still thunderstruck by this news.

"No. Did you want to be?"

"Not a chance in hell. It was the big reason I didn't want this party. I didn't want to make it real."

"Luckily for you, it's not. For two more years. Maybe, though, you've gotten it out of your system and won't freak out when it happens for real." Sarah's pinched face meant even she didn't believe it.

"Keep dreaming."

Sarah laughed.

"I feel even worse for getting mad at you about this," I confessed. "It's been lovely."

"It's not over. We're here for another five days. Maybe I can get you into the water." Sarah gave my shoulder a playful nudge, which set off a cascade of reactions inside me I'd almost forgotten.

"I'd rather get you alone for some naked cuddling and more," I told her, my tone deep and crackling with desire.

Sarah's eyes lit up. "Is that right? As it happens, Mom and Troy are letting us stay in their small cabin tonight."

"We'll have to change the sheets," I said before I could stop myself, no doubt killing the mood before I'd even had a chance to take advantage of it.

Sarah closed her eyes. "Don't ever change."

"Not sure I can, but I did pack something you might be interested in. In fact, I may have taken the opportunity a few days ago to add to my collection using a different account so it would actually be a surprise." My lips twitched. Now I had her full attention. "But first, cake."

"I'm not hungry for cake." Sarah's eyes devoured me, and suddenly, neither was I.

"Do you think anyone will notice if we slip away?" I looked around at everyone chatting. I may have been the guest of honor, but I was pretty sure no one would care if I disappeared for a while. Still, I didn't want to be rude.

"Do you really care?" There was a dare in her voice that did all sorts of delightful things to me. I had no idea why I'd let this part of me go dormant for so long, but I wasn't about to let this chance slip past me or to fall into bad habits again.

"Let's go," I growled, pinching Sarah's bottom before grabbing her hand.

I didn't glance in the cake's direction even once.

A HUGE THANK YOU

A HUGE THANK YOU!

First, thanks so much for reading Lizzie's stories. When I published the first book in the A Woman Lost series, I had no idea the impact Lizzie would have on so many. I've received countless emails from readers who have confessed how much Lizzie means to them.

I've published more than twenty novels, and I still find it simply amazing that people read my stories. When I hit publish on my first book back in 2013, after staring at the publish button for several days before I worked up the nerve to finally press it, I had no idea what would happen.

Ten years later, I still panic when I'm about to publish a new project, but it's because of your support that I find the courage to do it. My publishing career has been a wonderful journey, and I wouldn't be where I am today without you cheering me on.

If you enjoyed the story, I would really appreciate a review. Even short reviews help immensely.

Finally, don't forget if you want to stay in touch, sign up for my newsletter. I'll send you a free copy of *A Woman Lost* (just in case you don't have it yet), book 1 in the A Woman Lost series, plus the bonus chapters and *Tropical Heat* (a short story), all of which are exclusive to subscribers. And, you'll be able to enter monthly giveaways to win one of my books.

You'll also be one of the firsts to hear about many of my misadventures, like the time I accidentally ordered thirty pounds of oranges, instead of five. To be honest, that stuff happens to me a lot, which explains why I own three of the exact same *Nice Tits* T-shirt. In case you're wondering, the shirt has pictures of the different tits of the bird variety because I have some pride.

Here's the link to join: http://eepurl.com/hhBhXX

And, thanks again for letting Lizzie into your hearts.

ABOUT THE AUTHOR

TB Markinson is an American who's recently returned to the US after a seven-year stint in the UK and Ireland. When she isn't writing, she's traveling the world, watching sports on the telly, visiting pubs in New England, or reading. Not necessarily in that order.

Her novels have hit Amazon bestseller lists for lesbian fiction and lesbian romance. For a full listing of TB's novels, please visit her Amazon page.

Feel free to visit TB's website to say hello. On the *Lesbians Who Write* weekly podcast, she and Clare Lydon dish about the good, the bad, and the ugly of writing. TB also runs I Heart Lesfic, a place for authors and fans of lesfic to come together to celebrate and chat about lesbian fiction.

Want to learn more about TB. Hop over to her *About* page on her website for the juicy bits. Okay, it won't be all that titillating, but you'll find out more.

Printed in Great Britain
by Amazon